Bitcoin

AND THE FUTURE OF MONEY

JOSE PAGLIERY

TRIUMPH
BOOKS

This book is available in quantity at special discounts for your group or organization. For further information, contact:

Triumph Books LLC
814 North Franklin Street
Chicago, Illinois 60610
(312) 337-0747
www.triumphbooks.com

Printed in U.S.A.
ISBN: 978-1-62937-036-1
Book design by Alex Lubertozzi
Photo of Sapan Shah courtesy of Christa Neu, Lehigh University.
Photo of Josh Arias courtesy of Studio Moirae Photography.

To my wife, Bridget, who inspires me, guides me,
and always shows me there is a kinder, more noble way

We have progressively abandoned that freedom in economic affairs without which personal and political freedom has never existed in the past.

—Friedrich Hayek

Contents

Acknowledgments

I AM grateful to those within the Bitcoin community who were willing to share their stories with me. Remain true to your ideals. They are rooted in a desire for a better, freer world.

To my editor at CNNMoney, David Goldman, thank you for encouraging quality journalism. To CNNMoney's executive editor, Lex Haris, thank you for always pushing for clarity in my writing. And thanks to CNN for approving this. I am indebted to those at Triumph for this opportunity. Thanks to my friends who reviewed my writing and tested my logic.

I am grateful to my sister and mother for being models of strength. Mike, you pull me up when I fall. Sam Frade, you are my Doc Brown.

CHAPTER 1

Baby Steps

IT WAS an otherwise quiet news day in February when word got out that the niche online trading site Mt.Gox (mtgox.com) went offline. The difficulty for me then, as a technology and business reporter at CNNMoney, was to explain to the average reader how a website that few had ever heard of suddenly wiped out the savings of people around the globe. The loss totaled nearly $400 million at the time. And it was all in a currency no one understood, no less.

That was, for many people, the first time they'd heard of Bitcoin. The circumstances were less than ideal. But the occasion was an appropriate wake-up call.

The world was finally paying attention to the term *digital currency*. Put simply, it's electronic money—nothing more than bits in a computer, be it your laptop, smartphone, or some far-off computer server in a chilly, climate-controlled data center.

Make no mistake. It's real money. But it's unlike anything we've ever seen. Although it has similar properties to the paper bills we all carry in our wallets, a digital currency like Bitcoin is not printed by a recognized authority like a government that determines how many are put into public circulation. Nor is it valued in a traditional sense like gold, whose limited supply is slowly extracted from the earth at great labor and expense.

You can't feel or touch bitcoins. And it's precisely that aspect of a digital currency that polarizes people. Bitcoin's most idealistic supporters celebrate it as something akin to a monetary messiah, a means of exchange that will let you buy anything, anytime without nasty roadblocks, like banks or law enforcement. On the other end of the spectrum are the conservative cynics who think Bitcoin is bogus, nothing more than a money-making house of cards that's bound to fall as soon as the world wises up to the fact that zeros and ones on a computer are quite worthless.

They're both wrong. Bitcoin won't upend the world's super-powers—not entirely, anyway. But it's already leaving a lasting impact, because it represents a whole new way of thinking about money. Therein lies Bitcoin's promise. It has the potential to transform something that's a pivotal element of human history—shaking us to our very core.

To understand the significance of something like Bitcoin, it's worth doing a quick review of history. While economists and anthropologists disagree about the origin of money,[1] this much is certain: It's as old as human civilization. Money had already appeared by the time humans started jotting down the earliest surviving accounts of their actions in ancient Mesopotamia around 3100 BCE. At the time, it wasn't a medium of exchange in the form of gold coins or paper bills, though. It was merely a ledger of accounts, a running tally of who owes whom. But for all intents and purposes, the system of debt and credit served as a way to trade.

Some thinkers are inclined to say that money predates even government.[2] That's the argument put forward by free-market proponents like Adam Smith, widely accepted as the father of capitalism, and Austrian economist Carl Menger. Before the appearance of money, perhaps we bartered for goods. But bartering—or the credit system of ancient Mesopotamia—is a terribly inefficient way to trade.

The turning point came around 2000 BCE, when money appeared in a fashion more similar to what we know today. People in Egypt and Mesopotamia used receipts that showed how much grain they kept stored in temples. More than a thousand years later, metal coins gained ground in nearby areas. It eventually became too much of a hassle to lug around heavy sacks of misshapen bronze coins, so people everywhere opted instead for paper currency that represented value stored elsewhere, such as a bank. In China, they first appeared with merchants during the Tang Dynasty around 900 CE.[3] At about the same time in the medieval Islamic world, checks and promissory notes gained in popularity. Europe was the late bloomer, with paper currency making its first appearance in Sweden in 1661.

But that's just about where the story of monetary innovation ends. Surprising and disappointing, isn't it? Since then, governments have strengthened their control over the money-printing process, and countries continue to struggle with the fact that paper notes have no intrinsic value. This makes them susceptible to inflation, as occurs when a government prints extra bills to pay off its debts. That devalues its currency relative to others and impoverishes its people.

Meanwhile, banking has evolved many times over. The concept of a bank as we know it began in Italy during the Renaissance as a simple provider of bills of exchange, financing trade. Over time, banking has morphed to include loans, quick transfers of wealth across great distances, as well as a means of investing and consulting on those very investments. Over the centuries, banking has squeezed itself into the world of money, in the United States becoming the first and only entity to receive newly printed government dollars. Banks have placed themselves squarely between the people who earn money and the governments that issue it. They have made themselves necessary middlemen.

Indeed, in the modern era, banks have become synonymous with money and necessary for a prosperous life. Have you ever tried to conduct an expensive transaction without a bank? In most cases you'll get rejected or worse—a nasty glare from someone assuming you're up to no good. Or have you ever tried to receive steady pay for work in cash? Professionals will most likely receive a paycheck that needs to be cashed out at a financial institution, and some employers even make direct bank deposits mandatory. But think about what that does to society at large. It puts banks at the top of the social pyramid. Even though money is a necessary part of human interaction, something as ingrained in our consciousness as the rule of law, there exists an entity that retains firm control of it.

They are the gatekeepers. But that need not be the case.

Enter Bitcoin. For the first time in centuries, we're faced with a new kind of money. Because it runs on the Internet, this money can be sent across the globe in the blink of an eye with near anonymity. Anyone can receive it—and spend it—even if they live hundreds of miles away from their nearest ATM. And because it functions directly between one wallet holder and another, there are no banks that slow down the transaction process. No fees. No restrictions.

It sounds too good to be true. Or maybe we just forgot how liberating money is supposed to be.

CHAPTER 2

The Birth of Bitcoin

IT ALL started on an obscure online discussion forum dedicated to cryptography. The subject matter—the art of secure and secret communication—dictated that the regulars were mostly technical experts in mathematics and engineering. The "low-noise moderated mailing list" on metzdowd.com served as a de facto academic community, just the right place to introduce an experimental proposal that was equal parts economics and computer science.

It was Friday, October 31, 2008—Halloween, a day when millions don masks and hide their true identity. That's when the mysterious Satoshi Nakamoto first appeared with a message titled, "Bitcoin P2P e-cash paper" posted at 2:10 PM (ET):

> I've been working on a new electronic cash system that's fully peer-to-peer, with no trusted third party.
>
> The paper is available at: http://www.bitcoin.org/bitcoin.pdf

The nine-page, academic-style document described the fundamental details for a new currency and the unique, theoretical network to deliver payments. It detailed the complex way transactions would work, the heightened privacy offered to account holders and how the software would keep people from double-spending their digital coins.

The essay, "Bitcoin: A Peer-to-Peer Electronic Cash System" (see Appendix, p. 227), isn't a walk in the park to digest. But the introduction lays out a vision that's easy to grasp: Technological improvements have outpaced the development of financial networks, and we've outgrown the need for banks in the process. The main gripe for Nakamoto* was that banks have become a third wheel. They used to speed up transactions, but now they slow them down. As middlemen, banks settle payment disputes between buyers and sellers. To do that, they must charge fees. With those costs, it's not profitable for a bank to process tiny transactions, so we're limited in the kind of purchases we can make. Making matters worse, merchants fear customers might try to reverse a purchase, so they raise their rates too.

"What is needed is an electronic payment system based on cryptographic proof instead of trust, allowing any two willing parties to transact directly with each other without the need for a trusted third party," Nakamoto writes.

Nakamoto proposed a digital currency that would live on a network of computers, a well-meaning community willing to lend their machines' processing power to keep it alive. Together they would partake in a system that verifies transactions and "mines" for new bitcoins, producing electronic tokens at a steady rate. Bitcoin with a capital "B" would be the name of the new system; bitcoin with a lowercase "b" would mean the units of currency.

---

* There are many competing theories about the true identity of Satoshi Nakamoto. Aside from the usual "Is he Japanese or not?" there's also healthy debate about whether it's a man or a woman. It could be a single person or a group. For brevity and consistency, I'll abide by Nakamoto's own description and simply refer to the mysterious founder as "he." But I acknowledge it could very well be a trio of intelligent women at a secretive government agency.

The key to the entire system was something called a block chain. This was an innovative approach that simultaneously verified transactions, kept a log of them, and created new money. Users would mine for bitcoins by solving puzzles in segments called blocks. Those blocks would house publicly viewable information about recent transactions. A solved block would produce a unique code, or hash, that formed the foundation for the next block.

He was immediately peppered with highly technical questions and concerns from others on the mailing list. Could this system handle many simultaneous transactions? What would keep people from spending the same coin twice? After all, they're not physical. Such a blunder would topple the whole system. And what about nefarious hacker types who hijack whole server farms and turn them into spam-spewing zombies? Surely a system that lives on a network of volunteers' computers wouldn't stand a chance against that kind of coordinated attack.

Nakamoto's responses were careful, controlled, and respectful. A novel approach to verifying transactions would prevent someone from spending the same bitcoin twice, he explained. And the system, by relying on the combined computing power of lots of users, was designed to withstand any single attack of that kind.

The responses also revealed a great deal about him. He had a firm grasp of the most fundamental and often elusive characteristics of money. He was even more familiar with cryptography, having built the core functions of Bitcoin with the notion that new coins would be produced as computers solve increasingly difficult puzzles. But first and foremost, Nakamoto was a computer geek.

"I appreciate your questions," Nakamoto wrote. "I actually did this kind of backwards. I had to write all the code before I could convince myself that I could solve every problem, then I wrote the paper."

But there was something else. Beneath the highly technical language was a youthful idealism, a grand vision of what this opaque, unproven project could become. Nakamoto imagined that bitcoins could one day become popular enough that they would give birth to a new industry, one dedicated solely to maintaining much of the network and producing new bitcoins. By then, they'd be so desirable that hackers in control of server farms would rather use those slaves to mine for electronic money than attack the network or distribute annoying spam. At some point, the network would be large enough to easily handle the same kind of bandwidth seen by payment networks like Visa, processing tens of millions of transactions each day.

Above all, though, the system would be liberating. Although all transactions between digital wallets would be recorded in a public ledger, nameless wallets would allow for enhanced privacy, a sort of pseudo-anonymity. Without financial institutions taking a cut, it would be easier for people to make small, casual payments to one another. With a predetermined, controlled growth in the supply of electronic money built into the software, Bitcoin could avoid runaway inflation. It could become a go-to currency for people living under a government eager to print money and depreciating its own currency.

Bitcoin's rebellious nature and thinly veiled intentions didn't get lost on one commenter, who told Nakamoto point blank: "You will not find a solution to political problems in cryptography."

"Yes," Nakamoto replied. "But we can win a major battle in the arms race and gain a new territory of freedom for several years."

It was typical cypherpunk talk, derived from a school of thought that holds privacy sacred and personal liberties above everything else. In fact, understanding cypherpunk culture (not to be confused with cyberpunk, which is more of an art form) is key to appreciating Bitcoin and its enigmatic founder.

The name says it all. To use a cypher (or spelled correctly, cipher) is to convert information—say, a message to a friend—from its readable form into something incomprehensible, like a string of nonsense letters, numbers, and symbols. Using the right formula, you can take that indecipherable text and change it back into something readable.

It's quite empowering, when you think about it. The ability to communicate privately opens the ability to truly express your thoughts, to identify political or societal problems and criticize them without fear of retribution. That's particularly true as the Digital Age brings about the Information Age, when our means of communication via computers and phones have become practically seamless—as has the capability of governments and powerful corporations to spy on those conversations. We're all human, and barring the possibility that those in power are truly benevolent and infallible, securing our dialogues from prying eyes and ears is vital to maintaining any semblance of democracy—or any free and fair society.

But only rebels side against the powers that be. The punk part relates to their attitude. Ever since cypherpunks appeared as highly intelligent, computer-savvy activists in the 1980s, they've armed themselves with cryptography as a means for social change. In many cases, it's worked and keeps working. One early figure, John Gilmore, founded the Electronic Frontier Foundation, known as the world's top defender of civil liberties in the digital realm. Another is Philip Zimmermann, creator of the computer communication encryption method PGP, which stands for Pretty Good Privacy and is used by journalists and political dissidents around the globe to hide their communication from authoritarian governments. Another product of this school of thought is Tor, formerly known as The Onion Router, a special kind of software developed via funding from the United States Navy Research Laboratory that lets you surf online anonymously and access otherwise unreachable corners of the Web. Also among their ranks is Julian Assange, founder of the journalistic outfit WikiLeaks.

Most of these names and groups are familiar to those who pay attention to the tech world. But outside of that, they're mostly unknown. People are quick to acquire the latest smartphones, download the newest apps, and join social media networks, but they don't pay much attention to the activists toiling away to protect their privacy on those platforms.

Cypherpunks are insurgents, agitators, digital guerillas. Satoshi Nakamoto and Bitcoin fit right in.

"It's very attractive to the libertarian viewpoint if we can explain it properly," Nakamoto wrote in a post on November 14, 2008. "I'm better with code than with words though."

By that point, Nakamoto had been secretly working on his project for a year and a half, according to his messages to the tiny online community of cryptographers. That's telling. It would mean that this individual had started developing the electronic currency in the earliest days of the 2007 financial crisis.

Let's do a little time traveling. In the spring of 2007, New Century Financial Corporation, one of the top financial entities lending to folks with poor credit, collapsed under its own weight. It stopped accepting loan applications and, weeks later in April, filed for Chapter 11 bankruptcy protection.[1] It was among the first signs that subprime mortgage lending was doomed.

Then, over the summer, two credit rating agencies placed severe warnings on more than 600 bonds, because they were backed by subprime mortgages. From its New York headquarters, global investment bank Bear Stearns liquidated two hedge funds that had bet heavily on those types of loans. Members of the United States' central bank, the Federal Reserve, issued a stark warning that problems in the financial markets threatened the nation's economic growth. And the problems were global. In September, the Bank of England got approval to bail out the country's fifth-largest mortgage lender, Northern Rock.

The public was waking up to a grotesque reality. The levees guarding an otherwise conservative financial system had been broken for years, flooding us all with easy money that had been irresponsibly borrowed, lent, and traded on. Everyone was about to pay dearly for it.

In the United States, two major forces were at play. From one angle, government policies meant to increase access to loans, and therefore home ownership rates, had backfired. The once restrained landscape was now a risky one. The federal government had inflated a housing bubble through its support of Fannie Mae and Freddie Mac, two enterprises meant to ease access to home loans. Those two entities supported a secondary market for mortgages where they could be rounded up together, packaged, and sold to investors. And by propping up Fannie Mae and Freddie Mac with government-backed guarantees on loans, the federal authorities had vastly increased the supply of cash available to make home loans. There was an unintended result, however. To compete with these two entities, Wall Street banks created riskier types of loans.

From another angle, deregulation during the final years of the Clinton administration paved the way for banks to run amuck and drag us all down with them. The passage of the 1999 Gramm-Leach-Bliley Act repealed strict rules put in place after the 1929 stock market crash that led to the decade-long Great Depression. Gone were the provisions of the 1933 Glass-Steagall Act preventing everyday commercial banks, the ones holding all our precious home and business loans, from also becoming risky investment banks and insurance companies. In short time, we were all exposed to the whims of Wall Street bankers who knowingly traded in what was essentially garbage yet peddled out to the rest of the world as AAA-rated investments, the highest grade available.

The problem had several layers of complexity and points of failure. But many found the response by major governments even more appalling. Instead of letting irresponsible players pay the price for their own mistakes—banks, investors, and borrowers alike—governments moved in to bail them all out.

In the years since, the American people have had a difficult time accepting the narrative spun by politicians, central bankers, and their private banking brethren alike—that an economic disaster of apocalyptic proportions could only be avoided with a collective effort using public funds. And it's easy to see why. As government shored back support of schools and community programs, the money flowed for the very banks that helped put us in this mess in the first place.

We often forget the numbers, because they all came too fast, attached to stories too complex for the average reader and at a time when people were more focused on saving their mortgages than reading the newspaper. Here's a shortlist of the dozen biggest bailouts in the United States, rounded to the nearest billion, according to public interest news organization ProPublica.[2]

Entity	Total Disbursed
Fannie Mae	$116 billion
Freddie Mac	$71 billion
American International Group (AIG)	$68 billion
General Motors	$51 billion
Bank of America	$45 billion
Citigroup	$45 billion
JPMorgan Chase	$25 billion
Wells Fargo	$25 billion
GMAC (now Ally Financial)	$16 billion
Chrysler	$11 billion
Goldman Sachs	$10 billion
Morgan Stanley	$10 billion

Aside from two car manufacturers that naturally suffered from the fallout of the economic collapse, every entity on the list is a financial institution.

It was in the midst of this turmoil that Bitcoin was born, just as the failures of the modern banking system became apparent—as well as widespread disappointment in the politicians who enabled them and the regulators who failed to catch them. Our reliance on banks, middlemen that hoarded our cash and invested in risky assets, proved dangerous. And while the mass injection of money via bailouts and so-called quantitative easing by the Federal Reserve have not resulted in the hyperinflation many feared, there was a heightened state of distrust between the public and the bureaucrats controlling the nation's purse.

Meanwhile, in an unknown corner of the world, someone was developing a system that wouldn't have any of these problems. Bitcoin, as Nakamoto explained in the first essay, would be a trustless system without a need for trusted third parties:

financial institutions. The entire thing would live in a network that is peer-to-peer; that is, it would rely solely on the users themselves. They create the currency, they transfer it, and they keep it safe.

Safeguards would be built into the software of this computer program. To prevent widespread fraud stemming from people spending each electronic token twice, each transaction would carry a unique signature that gets time-stamped on a public ledger. The system would simply reject anyone trying to spend the same coin a second time. And while the list of transactions would remain public, people would still maintain relative anonymity, because only their wallet IDs—a long string of numbers and letters—would appear for all to see.

The network would be powered and regulated by the computers people use to access the system. Computational power from people's machines would be used to create new coins by solving intricate puzzles, and their computers' processors would also be harnessed to verify transactions in the public accounting book. In a nod to the lessons of capitalism, the system doesn't rely on the good nature of people, but instead on their selfish desires. If you help solve a puzzle and mine a new batch of bitcoins, you win a sort of lottery and keep your share of the proceeds. These puzzles would form the backbone to the entire system, because they would regulate how quickly coins could be created. To keep production steady and prevent inflation in their value, puzzles would increase in difficulty if computers started solving them too quickly.

This is how Bitcoin would eliminate the need for central banks that control the money supply and subject the populace to inflation. Gone as well are banks, payment card networks, and financial wire services, like Western Union, that take a cut of every transaction.

However, banks and credit card payment companies play another role for which people rarely give them credit. They form a buffer protecting most of us from fraud, siding squarely with consumers against merchants anytime there's a disagreement about a transaction. It's called chargeback, and it's the bane of every small business owner in the United States. Say you pulled out your credit card to purchase a television that never got delivered to your door. Complain to Visa or MasterCard, and they will immediately revoke the payment. The $500 that was once on its way to the bank accounts belonging to Big Al's TV Emporium is suddenly back in your possession. Lone entrepreneur Al Peabody is suddenly down $500 and has one less television in stock. The delivery service swears it sent the package, and its ongoing contract protects it from any liability.

Al still has to pay his hourly employees, so that money comes out of the cash flow he uses to restock the shelves. He hates the situation, but he's no match for the world's biggest financial giants. If he stops accepting credit cards, no one will buy from his shop. So instead, Al starts charging a few bucks extra on every television to account for the occasional chargeback.

A payment system like Bitcoin, which cuts out trusted third-party banks, has no place for chargebacks. That's a big draw for merchants, who can rest assured they will receive payment no matter what. That says a lot about the system's philosophy: Personal responsibility is paramount. There's no wiggle room for the sorts of shenanigans that thrived during the housing bubble that led to the 2007 financial collapse.

As Nakamoto wrote early on, "There's no reliance on recourse. It's all prevention."

Eventually, Nakamoto made good on his promise and delivered the actual Bitcoin software on metzdowd.com's cryptography mailing list. Here's part of the message he posted on Thursday, January 8, 2009, titled, "Bitcoin v0.1 released."

> Announcing the first release of Bitcoin, a new electronic cash system that uses a peer-to-peer network to prevent double-spending. It's completely decentralized with no server or central authority.
>
> See bitcoin.org for screenshots.
>
> Download link:
>
> http://downloads.sourceforge.net/bitcoin/bitcoin-0.1.0.rar
>
> Windows only for now. Open source C++ code is included.
>
>   - Unpack the files into a directory
>
>   - Run BITCOIN.EXE
>
>   - It automatically connects to other nodes

Evidence would later show Nakamoto had been running it for a few days. The software, Nakamoto warned, was still "alpha and experimental." As such, he offered no guarantees the system wouldn't be restarted. But he had built the software so that it could be updated and patched as necessary.

The system was designed to produce 21 million bitcoins total—no more, no less. It was a number he picked at random. At the time in 2009, mining for new bitcoins was the easiest it would ever be. The puzzles could be solved by the average PC in just a couple of hours. But as people joined the system, the puzzles would get more difficult and production would decrease over time. By its creator's calculations, the amount would be cut in half every four years, with 10.5 million tokens generated by 2013, another 5.25 million by 2018, then 2.625 million by 2023, and so on.

The electronic money could be sent in two ways. If your intended recipient was online, you could type in their computer's Internet Protocol (IP) address, the unique number assigned to each device connected to the net. If they weren't online at that moment, you could send tokens to their special Bitcoin address.

It all still sounded like an elaborate game, though. What made them any different from the brass Chuck E. Cheese play tokens embossed with "In Pizza We Trust?" At least those had a 25¢ play value you could reliably use at a skeeball machine.

"The real trick will be to get people to actually value the Bit-Coins [sic] so that they become currency," Dustin Trammel, a security researcher in Austin, Texas, said on the forum.

Nakamoto understood the concerns, but he didn't have a solid answer. After all, the value of bitcoins wouldn't be backed by anything tangible, like gold or the credit of a government. "It could get started in a narrow niche like reward points, donation tokens, currency for a game or micropayments for adult sites," Nakamoto wrote. "It might make sense just to get some in case it catches on. If enough people think the same way, that becomes a self fulfilling prophecy."

But at the time, there wasn't reason to get hung up on the debate about the actual value of a bitcoin. The important thing was to introduce something progressive. "I would be surprised if 10 years from now we're not using electronic currency in some way."

With that, Nakamoto left the discussion forum. It was time to shop around his idea.

———

On February 11, 2009, someone under the name Satoshi Nakamoto became a member at P2Pfoundation.net, an online community dedicated to peer-to-peer projects. He, she, or they never bothered to upload an image to his profile, but the person claimed to be a 36-year-old Japanese male. He hid his IP address and registered under satoshin@gmx.com, the same email used at the cryptography forum.

That same day, he posted a link to the newly created Bitcoin software program. One account tallied it at 31,000 lines of code. He had already mined the first batch of bitcoins, and hidden the following message within the "genesis block" of data:

> The Times 03/Jan/2009 Chancellor on brink of second bailout for banks

It was a reference to a news story that had just graced the Saturday cover of the *Times* of London—and a reminder of the very problems Bitcoin was meant to address.

This time around, the description was light on the highly technical talk about cryptography. Instead it was more tailored to the everyday folks who had recently grown bitter at the world's bank bailouts. In this description of the Bitcoin system, Nakamoto showed he had an axe to grind with fiat currency and fractional reserve banking.

It's worth taking a short detour to clear up the term *fiat* and provide a clear picture of how modern banking actually works. That will help explain Nakamoto's mission. Most people are under two major misconceptions about money and banking as they exist today. One is that paper money represents value stored elsewhere, such as gold in bank vaults. It doesn't. Money today is fiat money. These paper bills derive their value from the fact that a government mandates them. The word itself comes from the Latin term *fiat*, which roughly translates into the phrase "it shall be." This kind of money is desired, not so much because people want it, but because they're legally required to use it. And it's partly driven by fear. If your government forces you to pay taxes with it, you desire that currency because you don't want to end up in prison.[3]

Governments retain more power over their finances with this kind of money, because they can increase the supply of money at their leisure. Overwhelmed with debt to foreign nations? Just print more money to pay it off. The negative side effect is that each dollar is then worth less. But there's also a major benefit: If there's outside pressure threatening to wildly change the value of your country's dollar, your government is in a better position to counter the damage.

The other way to run things is with a gold standard, something the world loosely relied on for centuries until the 1970s. In that system, paper actually represents gold stored somewhere. It contrasts with fiat money in that gold-backed currencies don't let governments print bills at will without suffering immediate consequences. However, that system also subjects people to violent changes in prices as nations trade with one another and their physical stock of gold fluctuates.

The other misconception relates to the way banks work. Many people are under the impression that a bank takes the money you deposit there and uses it to make loans. Instead, banks make loans with money they don't actually have. That might sound confusing, but put bluntly, there's actually a legally permissible charade that goes on. It's called the fractional reserve banking system. In the United States, the largest banks are allowed to lend out 10 times the amount of money they actually keep in their vaults. When a bank approves a loan, the money merely blinks into existence on the borrower's bank account.[4] Doing so, banks essentially create money out of thin air.

The fractional reserve system makes it easier to access loans, because banks don't have to charge as much money to be profitable. It also turns banks that would normally be tiny, stingy Scrooges into massive powerhouses more inclined to give you money. The approach works until everyone asks for all their money back at once. Then it collapses.

Nakamoto told those at the P2P Foundation's website that Bitcoin could avoid the pitfalls of fractional reserve banking and fiat. First, there'd be no banks. And second, Bitcoin wouldn't be subject to the whims of central bankers, because new money is produced by software that sticks to a strict, reliable schedule. Nakamoto was tipping his hat to the approach to money supply voiced by Nobel Prize–winning American economist Milton Friedman, who suggested replacing the Federal Reserve with a computer.[5]

"The root problem with conventional currency is all the trust that's required to make it work," Nakamoto wrote. "The central bank must be trusted not to debase the currency, but the history of fiat currencies is full of breaches of that trust. Banks must be trusted to hold our money and transfer it electronically, but they lend it out in waves of credit bubbles with barely a fraction in reserve. We have to trust them with our privacy, trust them not to let identity thieves drain our accounts. Their massive overhead costs make micropayments impossible."

That same week, Nakamoto posted a similar message on SourceForge.net, a website where computer developers could upload free, open-source software for others to download. Archived numbers there show the growth was slow and steady. In the early days, Bitcoin didn't exactly go viral. In the first year or so, the program was downloaded by fewer than 60 people a month.[6] But word got out to key players in the tech space.

Computer programmers and tech-savvy finance experts willing to help advance the project reached out to Nakamoto.

Among the first was Hal Finney, a cypherpunk who was among the first to work on the PGP encryption method. He helped Nakamoto spot a few bugs in the software and on January 12 received 10 bitcoins (BTC) as a test, thus becoming the first ever recipient of a Bitcoin transaction.[7] Others joined in the months that followed.

Mike Hearn, an engineer at Google living in Zurich, Switzerland, extended a willing hand to Nakamoto in April of that year. A short time later, Jon Matonis, managing director at the electronic payment consulting company Lydia Group, did the same. In mid-2010, a self-described "code monkey" living in Amherst, Massachusetts, named Gavin Andresen offered to volunteer his C++ skills to fix any problems in the payment software. Nakamoto communicated with all of them, turning what was once a secretive venture into a collaborative endeavor involving dozens of technicians around the world.

All the while, the Bitcoin founder remained elusive and fiercely protective of his identity, dodging any questions about who he was, where he lived, or what gave him the skills to take on such an extraordinary undertaking. He never talked by phone. All correspondence was done via email or on pubic Bitcoin forums.

"I'm very curious to hear more about you," read Andresen's first message to Nakamoto. "How old are you? Is Satoshi your real name? Do you have a day job? What projects have you been involved with before?"

Nakamoto evaded them all. But he did accept the offer. "Great to have you!" he wrote back.

Over the next year, Andresen and others worked day and night to refine the software's code. While the Bitcoin network and its inner workings were nothing short of genius, the execution had its shortcomings. Parts of the code were sloppy by

Andresen's standards, according to interviews he gave in later years.[8] Even tiny mistakes could have huge consequences.

The first and—as of this writing—only major security flaw ever found in Bitcoin was discovered in August 2010.[9] Someone had managed to fool the Bitcoin software into producing more than 184 billion BTC in a transaction.[10] Nakamoto, computer developer Jeff Garzik, and others raced to address the problem, purging the transaction from the system's history and patching the hole.

As time went on, additional developers were brought in to address other issues with the code. Little by little, Nakamoto transitioned from the face of the project—albeit a masked one—into the background. By April 2011, he had successfully handed off the keys to Andresen, who in turn led a handful of other trusted technicians.

In a note to a developer, Nakamoto said he had "moved on to other things" and vanished.[11]

The next month, the Bitcoin software was downloaded 174,184 times from SourceForge.net. Another 329,229 did it in the month that followed. The world was catching on.

In those first two and a half years, Bitcoin went from being a completely unknown cryptography project to a niche online currency. Credit for that transformation belongs to exchanges— online trading platforms where outsiders unable to success- fully mine their own bitcoins could buy them for cash. The first to open was BitcoinMarket.com in February 2010.[12] That was followed in July by Mt.Gox (mtgox.com), a rebranded site that started out as "Magic: The Gathering Online Exchange," a hub where fans of the nerdy trading card game could buy and sell their wares.

It was amateur hour. Users frequently complained about scammers, compromised accounts, missed trades, and halted trading. But at least they could get in on the action. Mt.Gox rose to prominence, and in the latter half of 2010, the total value of all bitcoins being traded there reached an estimated $1 million.

Meanwhile, Bitcoin's popularity reached analysts at the Financial Action Task Force, an intergovernmental group that keeps a watchful eye on money laundering and terrorist financing activities. In October 2010, the organization noted the proliferation of digital currencies and warned about their ability to fuel illicit activities.[13] The report's writers were spot on. Within a few weeks, the website Silk Road was launched, creating a massive marketplace—running exclusively on Bitcoin—that functioned as an eBay for drugs.

The buzz around Bitcoin drove a surge in price that reached a notable point in February 2011, when it reached parity with the U.S. dollar. That caught the attention of *Time* magazine, which featured an article explaining how the currency was breaking new ground.[14] Major finance companies Visa, MasterCard, and PayPal had just shut off the flow of money to WikiLeaks, preventing the public at large from donating to the organization as retribution for its release of damning U.S. State Department diplomatic cables. But here was Bitcoin, this tiny, unheard-of currency that could circumvent the world's financial powerhouses and allow everyone to exercise their First Amendment rights—with their wallets.

But entering the Bitcoin world and keeping your electronic money safe was no less difficult than trying to survive a lawless town in a Spaghetti Western. Bad guys were everywhere. It was hard to tell the businesses from the bandits, especially when it became routine for them to shut their doors, claim a massive hack, and leave their customers empty-handed. MyBitcoin was among the first popular transaction processors, because its service was user-friendly. Naturally, it attracted those newest to the Bitcoin system. But they made for easy prey as well. In the summer of 2011, MyBitcoin announced it had been hacked, robbed of its 154,406 bitcoins and decided to shut down.[15] Their bitcoins were worth more than $2 million at the time, no small sum. Some customers said they reported the incident to the FBI, but little came of it. What should they have expected? The head of the site was a mysterious online persona known only as "Tom Williams." They had entrusted their bitcoins to a stranger—even though the system was specifically designed to eliminate third parties.

Slowly but surely, the world of Bitcoin drew in folks from all corners of the world. The first wave of privacy hawks and cryptography-obsessed mathematicians gave way to a crowd of computer programmers and Libertarians. Criminals and gold bugs soon followed. When the speculative investors and venture capitalists jumped in, major media outlets took notice.

Reporters began to ask who created this strange new technology. For journalists in the cross section between technology and business, finding Satoshi Nakamoto became equivalent to the mad archeological hunt for the Holy Grail. My favorite attempt came from Joshua Davis, who wrote a sweeping piece for the *New Yorker* in October 2011 that vastly narrowed down what kind of person would fit the description. Nakamoto used flawless English and occasionally used British spelling, with words like "colour" or "modernised." He spotted Nakamoto's reference to the *Times* of London. He spoke to Dan Kaminsky, an accomplished and world-renowned computer security researcher, who sketched this portrait: "Either he's a team of people who worked on this...or this guy is a genius."[16] The investigation took him to Crypto 2011, the absolute place to be for a cryptologist like Nakamoto, as well as those at the U.S. National Security Agency. There, Davis tracked down Michael Clear, one of the few from the United Kingdom in attendance, one who had graduated as a top computer science student at Trinity College in Dublin, worked on Allied Irish Banks' currency-trading software, and was an expert on peer-to-peer technology. Bingo. Clear rose through the ranks to become Suspect No. 1. Except, that is, for the caveat that the young man denied being Bitcoin's father—albeit with dodgy answers and a mischievous tone.

Alas, it wouldn't end there. The same feat was attempted by journalist Adam Penenberg at *Fast Company*, who used circumstantial evidence to point at three men who had filed a patent using an exact phrase from Nakamoto's white paper.[17] Information technology pioneer Ted Nelson, after reading a mystifying profile of Japanese mathematician Shinichi Mochizuki, identified him as the guy.[18] Vice reporter Alec Liu looped Bitcoin programmer Andresen, the federal government, and a few others into the mix.[19] Several toyed with the idea that Satoshi Nakamoto could be the joint project of electronics manufacturers SAmsung, TOSHIba, NAKAmichi, and MOTOrola.

But none of them were as explosive as the *Newsweek* cover story in March 2014.[20] The current affairs magazine had been absent from store shelves, and this was its big return to print. The cover was sexy as hell: a faceless man being unmasked. "The mystery man behind the crypto-currency," it promised. And boy, did it deliver a story. Senior staff writer Leah McGrath Goodman's hypothesis was poetic in its simplicity: Satoshi Nakamoto is actually Dorian Prentice Satoshi Nakamoto, a retired 64-year-old, Japanese-American model train collector in California who had, at one point, worked on secret projects for the U.S. military. On that fateful Thursday, March 6, reporters from all over Los Angeles descended on this poor man's home, demanding to know if he truly was Bitcoin's father. He offered a single Associated Press reporter an exclusive interview—to deny everything—and endured being chased across town by a mad convoy of cars and television trucks.

What got lost in all this frenzy? A small yet compelling detail. Bitcoin was, by design, an open-source project meant to be constantly updated, patched, and maintained by dedicated computer programmers. By the time journalists were shoving cameras into the face of this bewildered old man, more than 50 percent of the Bitcoin code had already been rewritten. Some put that figure closer to 70 percent.

Consider what that would have meant to a painting: Sure, some individual or group had stretched the canvas, sketched the piece, and laid down the oils with a paintbrush. But more than half of it had been completely reworked, with new layers coating the old ones, giving the work new life and brilliance.

Bitcoin's group of core developers made it clear to me how much of Nakamoto's initial programming had been reworked. It wasn't minor. In Garzik's words: "Satoshi was a brilliant designer, but not the best software engineer. Satoshi's code lacked standard software engineering practices such as a test suite, and was quite disorganized. We have refactored or rewritten a great deal of source code."

Bitcoin's lead developer, Wladimir van der Laan, told me Nakamoto's "original C++ code was hard to read and understand, and had quite a few (usually minor) bugs." It took hundreds if not thousands of volunteer hours from smart, dedicated computer geeks in love with Bitcoin to make up for those mistakes. They made it easier to use. And they continue to improve it with every passing day.

"It indeed doesn't matter who Satoshi is," van der Laan wrote to me. "If he/she/they would ever come back, they will have no special status in the project. By now there may be people that are more experienced and know more about Bitcoin and the underlying theory than Satoshi himself did. I don't claim that I do, though :)"

The project had, in no small sense, outgrown its founder. It belonged to the world now.

CHAPTER 3

Bitcoin Explained

SO HOW does it actually work? It helps to understand Bitcoin in two very different ways. One is to skim the surface and see how it mimics the real-life, physical money you already know. Thinking about it like an electronic coin helps explain how it's earned, used, and traded. But it's not exactly accurate. To truly comprehend Bitcoin, you have to accept what it really is: a network that runs on a computer program. The whole system is nothing more than ones and zeros stored in computers around the world. Everything relies on the software operating at the very core of it all: the block chain.

It's worth issuing a disclaimer: Bitcoin is electronic money, it's not money stored electronically. There's a major difference. Google Wallet, for instance, is a service provided by Google that stores your credit cards, debit cards, and loyalty cards. It's a digital wallet that holds on to your traditional money. But Bitcoin is a totally different approach. It reimagines what money actually is.

You'll need to get up to speed on a few terms that no sensible person uses in everyday life. They come from the world of cryptography, a dizzying environment of locks and keys, puzzles and solutions, secret messages and passcodes that reveal them.

Be patient. You won't need to remember everything. You can get along fine using bitcoins without memorizing all of it. But it's worth going over at least once. In fact, you'll likely come back to this chapter a few times, and the workings of the system will dawn on you over time. For me personally, it came in waves.

Let's start by getting a view of the whole picture. The Bitcoin network consists of computers that keep up the entire system and, for doing so, get rewarded in bitcoins. Users have digital wallets and trade bitcoins between one another. The system produces a fixed number of bitcoins every hour, and that number slowly dwindles over the years to max out at 21 million bitcoins. It's an arbitrary supply of money. There's no rhyme nor reason as to why the system tops out at that number. In any case, nearly 13 million were created by the spring of 2014. The last bitcoin is projected to be mined in the year 2140, if the system survives that long.

This section will go over all of the steps and players in the Bitcoin ecosystem: miners who dig for new bitcoins, exchanges where you can buy them, special wallets that let you store them and trade them. Everything is interconnected, so some things might not make sense at first. The true definition of a bitcoin doesn't even appear until later in the chapter. Don't get ahead of yourself. Just keep reading, and everything will tie together. You can find a more formal and rigorous explanation at the end of this book, which includes the pivotal white paper published by Nakamoto.

What Is a Bitcoin?

On a superficial level, you can think of bitcoin as a token. The previous page's image depicts the most widely accepted symbol, created as a mix between a capital letter *B* and the *$* sign. That symbol didn't exist in the Unicode standard used by computers when it was created, so an abbreviation is used instead: BTC. A single bitcoin is denoted as 1 BTC. It's digital, so it can be broken down into tiny numerical values—all the way down to eight decimal places. That means the smallest fraction of a bitcoin is 0.00000001, or one-hundred-millionth of a bitcoin (also known as a "satoshi").

Just as dollars are divided into pennies, nickels, dimes, and quarters, bitcoins are divided as well. Each portion has a different name:

1 BTC	a bitcoin
0.01 BTC	a bitcent
0.001 BTC	an mbit (pronounced em-bit)
0.000 001 BTC	a ubit (pronounced yu-bit)
0.000 000 01 BTC	a satoshi (named after Bitcoin's creator)

Just like a physical token, bitcoins can be in someone's possession. That owner can move them around, switching them to different personal wallets or handing them to someone else. Spending a bitcoin means you put it in someone else's possession.

Now let's apply this thinking to the digital realm. A bitcoin can be understood as part of a larger software system. Think of it as a computer file that is assigned to a certain owner's digital address (similar to an email address). It can only be moved with special permission. It also keeps a record of every place, or address, where it has ever been. That means it carries the history of every transaction in its existence.

But even that definition doesn't go far enough. At a more fundamental level, bitcoins appear as a section of data in a massive database. It's like a tally. There are entries on a public ledger. Any bitcoin that you "own" is really on that ledger. When you swap ownership, you hand over rights to that bitcoin. Your address merely points to that bitcoin, which remains on the block chain.

What Is the Block Chain?

At the heart of the Bitcoin system is the function that makes it tick. It's the true innovative contribution of this entire idea. Bitcoin's block chain is a record of all the transactions that have ever taken place, which are recorded in a chain of blocks.[1] Each block houses the latest group of transactions. And when you take the entire thing into account, it's a public ledger that details the history of every bitcoin. If a bitcoin ever changed ownership, that movement shows up on the block chain. It doesn't list people's names, though. It only shows digital wallets. Here's one example I randomly pulled from the popular website Blockchain.info, which lets you examine transactions:

As you can see, there's a certain degree of anonymity. Neither wallet shows anyone's true identity. But it's not right to call the entire system anonymous. If a wallet is tied to a specific person's name, the entire record of that person's wallet is easily available for anyone to see on the block chain. In that sense, it's the most transparent financial record the world has ever seen.

The block chain is maintained by participating computers, formally called "nodes," which verify the transactions in chunks called "blocks" and relay them across the network. This also involves solving an extremely complicated mathematical puzzle (for reasons I'll explain later). Anyone who downloads the Bitcoin software can become a node that helps sustain the system. It takes a lot of computing power and electricity, but there's a reason they volunteer. They're essentially "miners" who get rewarded in bitcoins.

How Are Bitcoins Created?

They technically come out of thin air. The software produces them and hands ownership to the lucky miner who first solved the puzzle. This is how the supply of bitcoins increases over time. Naturally, this lottery system attracts additional miners with more computing power. It's something of an arms race of powerful computing equipment, and miners even join forces to form stronger "mining pools" that split the winnings. Sound like a farce? Consider how serious people have gotten about this. The computing power dedicated to mining for bitcoins is equal to more than 1,400 times the combined computing power of the world's top 500 supercomputers.[2] And it's only getting bigger. But Nakamoto saw this coming. To prevent them from figuring out the puzzles too often and having the money supply rise too quickly, there's a speed limit built into the software. Every two weeks (or 2,016 blocks), the difficulty of the mathematical problem increases to ensure that one block gets added to the block chain every 10 minutes or so. That's also the time it takes for a transaction to get approved. Here's what the increasing difficulty looks like over the course of a year:

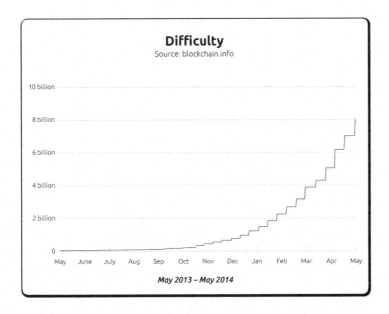

Difficulty
Source: blockchain.info

May 2013 – May 2014

As of 2013, a miner who solves a block gets rewarded with 25 bitcoins, but that too gets smaller over time. Every four years (or 210,000 blocks), the reward gets cut in half. In 2017 the prize gets cut down to 12.5 bitcoins. Here's what Bitcoin production will look like over time:

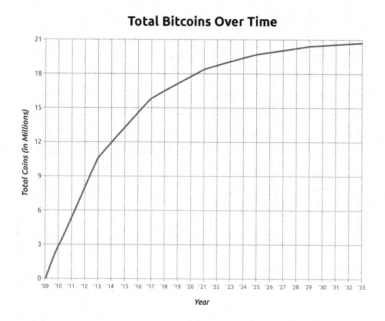

Total Bitcoins Over Time

As shown above, an estimated 98 percent of them should be produced by 2030, and the total number of available bitcoins will increase very slowly after that.

How Are Bitcoins Stored and Moved?

Bitcoins are kept in digital wallets that function like a bank account. You can move funds in and out. Anyone who knows the address can deposit funds into it, but only a person with the right permissions can make withdrawals. And you can keep it locked out of reach, or accessible to others. It all depends on a special system of public and private keys.

A wallet is an encrypted computer file, and it communicates with other wallets using something called public key cryptography.[3] In the computer world, it's the tried and true method for securely transmitting information. It's quite complicated. But it's easily understood with an analogy.

Imagine you want to send a sensitive letter to a friend by physical mail. Licking an envelope shut just won't do. Any postal worker can just open it and see what's inside. But they can't open a lock. So you ask your friend to buy a padlock, open it, and send it your way. He keeps the key. Once you receive his lock, you put your letter inside a box and close it shut with your friend's lock. Send it to him. Now he can open it with his private key, which never left his possession. This is called an asymmetric key system, and its major strength is that you never need to send keys to one another. You just share a lock—which can't be used to open boxes anyway.

Here's how that applies to Bitcoin. Anyone can create a digital wallet. The identifying code is long enough that, in real terms, they'll never run out. Every digital wallet is assigned a public key (the lock) and a private key (the key). Your public key doubles as your address. You can share your public key to receive incoming bitcoins. That's like announcing your bank account number. That address looks something like this: *1HcZyBdd53zbtoAUvUGSw1YaqTCLEA4079*. It lets anyone deposit money into your account. But you never share your private key, because that authorizes transactions out of your wallet. It's like handing someone your secret password. That can empty your wallet in a flash.

Conversely, if you want to send bitcoins out of your wallet, you'll need your friend's public key. But you'll still need your private key to authorize that outbound transaction. Think back to our postal mail analogy. When you send bitcoins to another person's digital wallet, you're essentially saying this: "Whoever has the private key that corresponds to this address can spend this money."

This is also why you never want to forget your private key. If you lose that, the bitcoins in your wallet will stay stuck there forever. You can see them, but you can't do anything about it.

The public/private key system is secure, but only if you keep your private key secret. There's a certain degree of risk to keeping the text file with your private key on a computer that's Internet-accessible. If you click on the wrong link and accidentally download malware, a hacker could scan your computer for a Bitcoin wallet, find your private key and empty your account. There are generally two different ways to store your bitcoins.

A hot wallet: This means your public and private keys are stored on a device that's connected to the Internet or an online service like a Bitcoin-trading exchange (more on that later). It's the most convenient way to store your bitcoins, because they're easily accessible. It's the equivalent of keeping cash on you as you walk down the street. However, like in real life, this practice is not the safest. Your stash is at risk, because your private key is lying around somewhere on your computer, smartphone, or in the case of an online exchange, in that company's servers. If a hacker ever gets access, your bitcoins are as good as gone.

Cold storage: As you could guess, this means the opposite of a hot wallet. Keeping bitcoins in cold storage means that the public and private keys are stored offline. There's no chance a hacker can spy on you. There are several ways to achieve this, because public and private keys are nothing more than a string of letters and numbers. You could keep them saved on a USB stick. Or you could save them on a portable hard drive. But the problem with either of these is that if your hardware malfunctions and stops working, that's it. You've lost everything. That's why your best bet is to print them out on paper, and fold that paper shut. Obviously, you don't want to snap a photo of that and keep it on your phone or computer (which are connected to the Internet). Some people even inscribe their public and private keys into metal, which is less likely to fade over time than ink on paper. You can print your keys on a metal dog tag necklace if you want. Cold storage is by far the most secure way to keep your bitcoins, because it's easier to keep them out of others' reach. If you are so inclined, you could use multiple layers of security, keeping your bitcoin keys in an encrypted file on a hard drive in a locked safe. A thief would need to know the physical location of your safe, its lock combination, the password to your hard drive, and the passcode to your encrypted file.

The smartest approach is to mimic what you do in real life, carrying enough cash for everyday activities and keeping your savings in the bank. In Bitcoin terms, that means keeping most of your digital currency in cold storage, and occasionally moving small portions to a hot wallet. Because of the curious way bitcoins are transferred from wallet to wallet, your cold storage can receive bitcoins anytime—even though it's never connected to the Internet. Remember, you can receive bitcoins as long as the sender knows your public address. You can share your cold storage wallet's public key, and keep receiving bitcoins, even though you never connected that wallet to the Internet. Sound odd? Remember, Bitcoins never actually move. They're never technically in your possession. They're always on the block chain.

Bitcoins Never Move?

Nope. This is where the similarities between the physical world and digital realm must end. Brace yourself. To gain a true understanding of how Bitcoin works, you have to come to terms with this fact: The block chain is everything. It's a record of every bitcoin transaction ever made. And that's incredibly important, because there is no such thing as a bitcoin.

But I've Seen Photos of Bitcoins!

Those aren't actual bitcoins. They're akin to a paper wallet. Somewhere on the physical coin or inside it are written a pair of keys.

Bitcoins Don't Exist?!

There is no entity, no string of code, no computer file that you can identify as a bitcoin. All that exist are Bitcoin addresses (public keys) and records of inflows and outflows. If the entire block chain has two mentions of your public key—one that says your address received 1 BTC, and another that says it received 2 BTC—that means you own 3 BTC. But you can't point to a line of code and say, "That there is my bitcoin." That information lives on the database. Your public and private keys merely point to a section of the block chain.

That's why you can "keep" bitcoins in a wallet whose private key is jotted down on something that's not connected to the Internet. As long as you create a public key that exists on the block chain, you can be sure that it can receive incoming bitcoins. At this point, it becomes clear that Bitcoin isn't truly the trading back and forth of virtual coins. It's all about the backbone of a computer network. And it only exists this way. If the network disappears, Bitcoin ceases to exist. This is why bitcoins can't be counterfeited. There are no bitcoins to move.

To understand why the system is designed this way, think about what would happen if a bitcoin were a standalone computer file. Digital things can be copied. If a bitcoin were a string of code, like a byte that lives in a computer, anyone could counterfeit bitcoins and make their own. But if all that exists is a shared database of transactions, and everyone says you received a bitcoin, then by all accounts you "own" a bitcoin. Even if you've never held it, seen it, or had it in your possession. And you can't just decide on your own to make your own bitcoin, because the shared database doesn't show a record that you received any. If the block chain says you were never transferred any bitcoins, you don't own any bitcoins.

Then How Are Bitcoins Transferred?

Remember, everything happens on the block chain.[4] Miners everywhere are keeping that block chain alive. And the block chain keeps a record of every transaction. This is how they all come together.

Let's say you want to send a friend a bitcoin. You need his public key (to know where to send it) and your private key (to sign off on the deal).

When you use your private key, you're actually doing two things. First, you're linking it up with your public key and announcing to the Bitcoin network that you're authorized to do the transaction. Click. It's a working key pair. Second, you're digitally signing a "hash"—a shortened code version—of the previous transaction. This is what keeps a perpetual record of every bitcoin movement. Inside every transaction is a record of the last one. That's why Nakamoto defined a bitcoin as "a chain of digital signatures."

Now you've broadcasted the proposed transaction across the Bitcoin network. It's up to the nodes, those miners, to make it official. This is the part that makes Bitcoin so revolutionary. Instead of relying on a bank or credit card company to verify that you're spending money that's truly in your possession, the entire Bitcoin system relies on independent miners around the world. It's up to the "nodes" of the network to ensure you're not spending the same bitcoin twice.

Your proposed transaction is time-stamped and gets in line behind many others. They're rounded up together in a group of transactions, called a block. If the system figures out that all those transactions are valid (no double-spending the same coin), the block gets approved and joins the block chain. All the transactions inside that block have been set in stone. The deal is done. The bitcoin is now in your friend's possession.

Your transaction takes 10 minutes to get verified. Again, remember that each block takes about 10 minutes. Your transaction isn't verified until that block makes it into the chain. That means there's a period of obscurity in which transactions haven't settled. There's a window of opportunity to send the same coin in two different directions. It will only end up in one of them. In essence, there's a real-life delay if you want to make sure the deal went through.

So What Exactly Are the Miners Doing?

Let's stop calling them "miners" for a moment. Just think of them as computers that do two things. One, they group proposed transactions together into blocks and send them out to others on the network. Two, they look through blocks to verify that all the transactions inside them are legit. Once a block is approved, it gets added to the official block chain.

A lot of this requires a special process called hashing, so it's worth getting a firm grasp of what this means. Recall that a hash is simply a code. How does this happen? A mathematical algorithm is applied to a concept, like a word, and it translates that information into a code of a fixed length. If any part of that word changes, the hash changes too. So each object has a unique hash. I've applied a special type of hash to a few words below. I used a special hash function developed by the U.S. National Security Agency called the Secure Hash Algorithm. This one in particular is SHA-256. Note that no matter how many letters the input is, the result is always the same length.

Input   **Hash Function**   **Result**

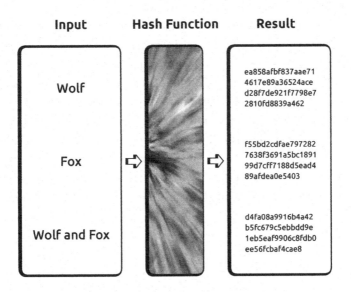

Wolf

ea858afbf837aae71
4617e89a36524ace
d28f7de921f7798e7
2810fd8839a462

Fox

f55bd2cdfae797282
7638f3691a5bc1891
99d7cff7188d5ead4
89afdea0e5403

Wolf and Fox

d4fa08a9916b4a42
b5fc679c5ebbdd9e
1eb5eaf9906c8fdb0
ee56fcbaf4cae8

Now back to Bitcoin. Your computer's first job is creating blocks. Think of blocks as a box of information. Creating a block is hard work with a lot of things going on at once:

- Your computer gives the block a version number.
- Remember that transactions between Bitcoin users get broadcasted to the network. Your computer packages all the recent proposed transactions together and creates a hash to represent them all.
- It issues a time-stamp.
- It grabs information from the most recent, finalized block on the block chain, and it hashes that too.

- It creates a random variable called a "nonce."

In real life, a nonce is a made-up, one-time-use word created to describe something. For example, in the movie musical *Mary Poppins*, she uses the word "supercalifragilisticexpialidocious" to define a special moment. Similarly, your computer uses a nonce because it's presented with a special problem. Every time a block is put together, the entire block is given a unique hash. So, when the nonce changes, the block's hash changes too.

Here's the problem bitcoin miners solve with a nonce: They have to end up with a certain kind of hash for each block. It has to have just the right number of zeros at the beginning. So your computer keeps spitting out a new nonce repeatedly until it gets just the right hash for the block.[5] The more computing power you have, the faster you can try new nonces, and the faster you can solve for the latest block. This is what a block hash looks like:

```
000000000019d6689c085ae165831e934ff763ae46a2a6c172b3f1b60a8ce26f
```

Once your computer has created a block hash that works, it broadcasts that out to the network of computers. This is when a computer's second job comes in: examining the blocks that have been broadcasted. Now it's up to everyone else to verify that you did it correctly. The other computers on the Bitcoin network scan your submission and check to make sure it has all the right parts.[6] Here are some key points. You'll note it looks very similar to the list we already covered:

- The time-stamp has to be recent.
- Your proposed block has to show that it was built on top of the real block chain, so it has to contain the right hash for the most recent, finalized block on the block chain.

- All of the transactions inside the block must be valid. A single person could not have spent the same bitcoin twice. This must be the first time an owner is using their special digital signature to pass that bitcoin along.

If another person's computer approves your block, it starts working on the next one and relies on your block as the "previous block hash." One by one, this quickly happens across the Bitcoin network. When a majority of the network's CPU power decides that your block is the previous one, it's official. Your block is part of the block chain. It's a democratic process.*

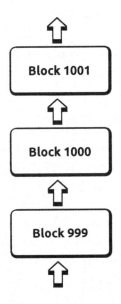

You get a reward for all that rapid-fire nonce-guessing and picking out the right one. The Bitcoin system sends a certain

---

* This also means that if any entity, such as a mining pool, gets more than 50 percent control of the network, it can make unilateral decisions about accepting blocks or not. It essentially becomes an authoritarian Bitcoin central bank.

number of bitcoins in your direction. Currently, it's 25 BTC. That's why this process is calling mining. Your computer exerts effort, and as a result, bitcoins appear.

How Does the System Control the Supply of Bitcoins?

Miners solve a puzzle that gets increasingly difficult. Your block's hash has a certain value.[7] The Bitcoin protocol presents a target value, and your goal as a miner is to produce a hash that has a smaller value than that target. But remember, all you can do is keep guessing nonce variables and randomly generating hashes. As the target value gets lower, it gets harder to guess the right one. It's a game of mathematical limbo: How low can you go?

The difficulty of the game is adjusted every 2,016 blocks to ensure that a new block gets added to the block chain every 10 minutes or so.

Why All the Hashing?

This isn't just happening to give you a headache. There are two main reasons. One is that it keeps the block chain from blowing up with too much information at every step of the way. Each block is stacked on top of the previous one. If each block needed to read all of the text of the previous block, the amount of data would quickly balloon out of control. Hashing allows you to condense the data. It's kind of like looking at a single fossil and being able to determine the entire history of a species.

The other reason is that there's an added layer of security. It's unfathomably difficult—essentially impossible right now—to slip incorrect data into the block chain. Anything even slightly off by a single letter would change a hash and get rejected. And the more hashing that happens, the taller the layers get. It's creating a passcode of a passcode of a passcode.

This Is Too Theoretical. What Does a Block Look Like?

You asked for it. Here's the so-called "genesis block," the first one ever created.[8] Unless you're a cryptographer with serious computer skills, this is absolute nonsense.

```
{
    "hash":"000000000019d6689c085ae165831e934ff763ae46a2a6c172b
    3f1b60a8ce26f",
"ver":1,
"prev_blok":"00000000000000000000000000000000000000000000000000
0000000000000000",
"mrkl_root":"4a5e1e4baab89f3a32518a88c31bc87f618f76673e2cc77ab
2127b7afdeda33b",
    "time":1231006505,
    "bits":486604799,
    "nonce":2083236893,
    "n_tx":1,
    "size":285,
    "tx":[
        {
"hash":"4a5e1e4baab89f3a32518a88c31bc87f618f76673e2cc77ab2127
b7afdeda33b",
        "ver":1,
        "vin_sz":1,
        "vout_sz":1,
        "lock_time":0,
        "size":204,
        "in":[
            {
                "prev_out":{
"hash":"00000000000000000000000000000000000000000000000000000000
000000000000",
                "n":4294967295
            },
"coinbase":"04ffff001d0104455468652054696d65732030332f4a616e6
2f32303039204368616e63656c6c6f72206f6e206272696e6b206f6620
7365636f6e64206261696c6f757420666f722062616e6b73"
        }
    ],
    "out":[
        {
            "value":"50.00000000",
 "scriptPubKey":"04678afdb0fe5548271967f1a67130b7105cd6a828e
03909a67962e0ea1f61deb649f6bc3f4cef38c4f35504e51ec112de5c384df
7ba0b8d578a4c702b6bf11d5f OP_CHECKSIG"
        }
    ]
}
],
    "mrkl_tree":[
        "4a5e1e4baab89f3a32518a88c31bc87f618f76673e2cc77ab127b7
        afdeda33b"
    ]
}
```

Does Block Creation Ever Go Wrong?

Sometimes. All this stacking of blocks on top of one another is a complex game, and once in a while, things get confusing. It's like digging tunnels in the wrong direction. At some point, you're forced to pick up, walk over to the right spot where your buddies are, and restart digging.

For example, sometimes two Bitcoin miners solve a puzzle at nearly the same time. They won't both have their blocks join the block chain. The system will select only one of them, let's call it Block A, and the block chain will continue getting built on top of Block A. The other, Block B, is a road to nowhere.

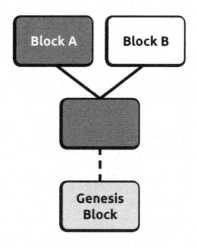

But some computers might start mistakenly building on top of Block B. Any subsequent blocks are called "orphan blocks." Everyone on that detour is wasting their time, because their confirmation won't make it into the true block chain. This is why the Bitcoin protocol enforces a waiting period before miners can spend the bitcoins they generated on their own. Their reward counts as a transaction, and that transaction needs to be confirmed 100 times, or about 16 hours. The valid blocks are in dark gray.

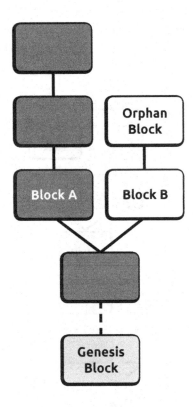

The rules written into the Bitcoin software keeps the block chain from forking in different directions forever. Eventually, the misguided computers on the network will switch back to working on top of the longest chain of blocks—naturally, the original one that dates back to the genesis block. When that happens, the detoured miners' rewards disappear. Their rewards don't appear on the true block chain, so they have earned no bitcoins for their work. Remember, the block chain's transaction history is everything. Also, all the transactions that were confirmed by the detoured miners are put into a queue on the real block chain.

Putting all of that together, this is what the block chain looks like in its totality. Again, the valid blocks are dark gray:

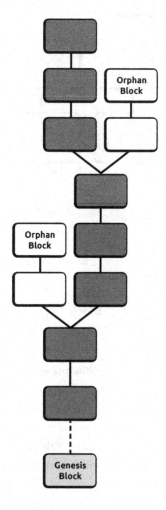

How Can I Start Mining?

You'll need to download what's called the "full Bitcoin client." It's free and open source, which means that it's maintained by a dedicated group of volunteer computer developers. The only website I recommend is Bitcoin.org, the official home of Bitcoin. The Bitcoin mining program works for all popular operating systems: Linux, Mac, and Windows.

The software hooks up your computer to the network and turns it into a node. You will become a full member of the Bitcoin community, contributing to its well-being and maybe even scoring some bitcoins. However, nowadays earning bitcoins is highly unlikely, because this has become a professional endeavor. Companies are sinking millions of dollars into building massive collections of powerful computers called server farms that are solely dedicated to mining bitcoins.

If you're going to do it anyway, be patient. Your computer needs to download the entire block chain, which stands at more than 16 gigabytes as of May 2014. That's equivalent to about 3,200 mp3s, so expect the initial synchronization with Bitcoin Core to take all day and night.

How Do I Just Get a Digital Wallet?

There are many free wallet software programs available, and they all generate wallets that can hold on to, send, and receive bitcoins. It's all a matter of where you want to manage this wallet. Desktop wallets only work on desktop computers, and they tend to be much larger wallet programs that require more computing power. Mobile wallets are meant for your smartphone and work as lightweight apps. Web wallets are accessible via any Web browser, so they can work from your computer, tablet, or any Internet-connected device.

There are several types of desktop wallets, and many can be found at Bitcoin.org. Non-technical people might like the wallet program MultiBit, which has a reputation for working quickly and being easy to use. It operates in several languages and works with all major operating systems. The wallet program Hive was designed for Mac OS X. Then there's Armory, which offers additional security features for Windows and Linux users. A fourth option is Electrum, which runs on servers and is versatile because the same wallet can be accessed from different computers.

There are several types of mobile wallets, and it's not recommended to download just any app from your phone's app marketplace. Hackers tend to lurk in such places, and they could easily dupe you into downloading malware or an infected version of a wallet program. Instead, head to Bitcoin.org and see what's there. The website currently features two types. The official Bitcoin Wallet app runs on Android and BlackBerry devices. A third-party application called Mycelium works only on Android phones. It's worth noting that Apple blocked all Bitcoin wallets from its App Store in a move that was perceived as corporate bullying by the Bitcoin community. iPhone users were forced to instead rely on Web wallets, which are accessible via the iPhone's Safari Web browser. Apple later went back on its decision and, in mid-2014, started to allow Bitcoin services once again.

There are several wallets, and they all essentially offer a similar service. You'll want to check these out, and others, on your own: Blockchain.info, BitGo, GreenAddress.it, Coinbase, and Coinkite.

Where Can I Get a Bitcoin without Mining?

Unless you receive a bitcoin as a gift, you'll have to buy one. This process is explained at length in the next chapter. However, the easiest way is to buy them at online exchanges. These are virtual trading floors that operate like Wall Street trading floors. Sellers and buyers come together, negotiate prices, and swap them. The sole purpose of keeping your bitcoins on an exchange is to continue buying and selling bitcoins. Otherwise, you can just acquire them, then send them to your own digital wallet, and store the keys in a secure place.

What Gives a Bitcoin Its Value?

Nothing gives a bitcoin value except that people want them. Unlike government-issued dollars, there is no legal requirement to accept bitcoins as payment. And unlike precious metals like gold and silver, which are desired as jewelry and used for industrial purposes, there is no use for bitcoin other than money or a speculative investment at the moment. Put plainly, Bitcoin isn't rooted in anything traditionally considered valuable. That's one of the reasons the price of a bitcoin is highly unstable.

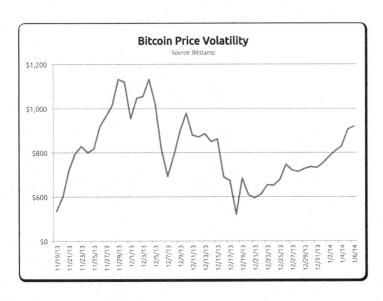

The other is that the entire system depends on brand-new, unproven technology that was developed mysteriously. It's no wonder that people are wary of it and owners of bitcoins get scared at the slightest impression there's something wrong with the software. Worries trigger sell-offs at exchanges, and the price of a bitcoin drops like a meteorite.

Still, that doesn't discourage people from hooking up their computers and becoming nodes in the Bitcoin network. In May 2014, there were 7,661 nodes connected to the system on a Saturday night, with half in the United States, Canada, and Germany (in descending order).[9] At the same time, Blockchain.info counted 1.5 million users of its digital wallet, a number that has been growing steadily for more than a year—and that's just one company. We've covered how the Bitcoin world works in theory. Now it's time to see how it actually works in real life.

CHAPTER 4

Using It in Real Life

JAMES KAFKA is a master of machines that produce things the average person would find inconsequential. By night, the 31-year-old stands by behemoth printing machines that tower above his 6′3″ frame. He's the commander in charge of this full-color ink-cartridge tank battalion, but sometimes it feels like the other way around. They spit out a steady stream of papers, and he's there to slice them. They keep coming. He keeps cutting. He's sheared so many, there's a good chance you've gotten one. Then again, you probably threw it away without taking a second look. It's junk mail. But Kafka doesn't mind. It's tolerable and pays the bills—so he can tend to the machine he really loves.

A brand new Sapphire Radeon HD 5830 graphics card doesn't come cheap. Neither does a Radeon HD 7970. Together, these tiny, odd-looking boxes easily fetch $600. And good luck finding a new one. Most major retailers don't even list their prices, because they're out of stock. But Kafka managed to get his hands on both and loaded them into his Frankenstein computer at home in the Philadelphia suburb of Lansdale, Pennsylvania. The extra muscle turned it into a PC on steroids. The home-built rig gets so hot, he had to install an awkward-looking, 20-inch window fan on it just to keep it cool. In the snowy winter, he even leaves it on the covered porch of his home. It runs 24/7, crunching numbers and racing to solve the next Bitcoin crypto puzzle, sucking up energy like a colossus. This is the machine he tends to by day. This is the life of a Bitcoin miner.

Kafka got into it a few years ago, after hearing about Bitcoin through his sister's friend and spotting a few curious posts on the forum website Reddit. Back then, he spent most of his free time sitting at home and playing Eve Online, commanding space cruisers and fighting interstellar battles. He was devoted enough to the Internet gaming community that he built a PC from scratch to maximize the experience. But when he wasn't blowing up enemy frigates and freighters, all that computing power was going to waste. So he decided to let it mine for bitcoins. When the coins started coming in, Kafka got hooked. Sure, this electronic money wasn't worth much, maybe a few bucks here or there. Kafka recalls thinking "it was just magic Internet money." But as the price went up, this play money became an effortless income stream. The computer did all the work. He gave it some more muscle by installing a $130 graphics card, and all of a sudden, traveling through interstellar wormholes didn't seem as rewarding as earning bitcoins.

"Once you're mining, you pretty much can't do anything else," Kafka told me. "I would only stop mining if I needed to do something on the Internet."

And he kept that to a minimum. Kafka fine-tuned his hardware to run at maximum capacity, twice pushing it so far that he fried his graphics card. He would then spend some of the real-life physical cash he earned working at the printing shop to replace gear that earned him digital money he couldn't really spend anywhere. It sounds futile, but it felt good. Kafka knew he was on the cutting edge of something special, almost like he was in on a big secret before the rest of the world caught on to it. He teamed up with a friend; they joined a larger pool with other miners, and the guys agreed to split the proceeds.

It's been a rocky road. The hobby barely pays for itself. In March, Kafka broke just about even, earning close to half a bitcoin for himself and paying $270 in electricity. That doesn't account for the cost of hardware, which needs to get replaced whenever it goes down—or when it never arrives. In 2013 Kafka experienced firsthand how flaky the Bitcoin world can be. He came across TerraHash.com, a website that marketed itself as a maker of specialized Bitcoin-mining hardware. Kafka and his buddy spent their entire stockpile, 11 bitcoins worth about $1,200, on two microchip sets. Forget the hobby stuff. This was a calculated capital outlay.

"We told ourselves, 'We've gotten somewhere. Let's reinvest,'" Kafka recalled. "We ran the numbers, and they were going to produce more than that. They would return our investment in six months, and anything after that was profit."

Except it never arrived. The TerraHash website stopped updating its blog on September 5 that year, and Kafka joined the scores of people online who claimed they preordered equipment that hadn't shipped. He even looked up the business registration, found a California address, and considered flying out there to ask for his money back, but decided against it. Adding to the sting: he paid in bitcoins, which meant he couldn't just cancel the charge like he could with a credit card.

"It was poetic, ironic, ridiculous," he told me nearly a year after that episode. "I'm sitting here mining bitcoins, paying in Bitcoin, and I'm completely screwed out of my money. I said, 'I'll never try to order mining hardware with bitcoin again.' At this point I can laugh about it. But it's a cautionary tale for other people. Make sure you know what you're getting into."

"Do you feel like you do?" I asked.

"Sometimes," he said with a chuckle. "It is the Wild West. There have been bitcoins stolen here, stolen there, people doing pumps and dumps. It's unbelievable. It's not illegal to steal someone else's money. That's the only thing it teaches me. I'm not going to go out and steal bitcoins, but there's no legal recourse for this stuff."

But Kafka and his friend are still at it, lugging their computers to the frozen porch in the winter and down into the cool basement in the summer, keeping an eye out for good deals on top-of-the-line graphics cards and constantly monitoring electricity costs. His friend is always calculating and analyzing, trying to ensure they never spend more than they rake in. But they do eat the costs in real cash. They've saved every bitcoin since their 11-bitcoin snafu, so the monthly $500 or so comes out of their pockets. It's not easy. To deal with the costs, Kafka has dialed back his spending habits. He ditched his AT&T contract and iPhone for an off-brand device and a flat-rate Virgin Mobile plan. He switched to a cheaper car insurance plan too. He even quit his $7-a-day smoking habit—all for the love of Bitcoin. His girlfriend doesn't mind, and his family kindly listens as he preaches about it at gatherings.

"I'm never going to be a multimillionaire from doing this," Kafka said. "If I can make a little money, it's cool. I'm having fun doing it. It just feels like the bleeding edge. It's exciting to see where it's going to land."

———

There are Bitcoin millionaires, though. They're a rare bunch blessed by an odd serendipity. These types got into Bitcoin early, sometime in 2009 or 2010, and quietly amassed a collection of thousands of bitcoins when they were still going for nickels and dimes. By late 2013, as the price of a bitcoin briefly pushed past $1,000 a pop, they sold off some or most of their stash. I've spoken to a few of them, and they tend to be highly guarded and private. To them, the experience was akin to winning the lottery—and they don't want their middle-class friends to know their financial secret. But one Norwegian man's experience captures this beautifully.

Kristoffer Koch was a college student at the Norwegian University of Science and Technology in 2009 when he stumbled on Nakamoto's initial paper on Bitcoin.[1] At the time, he was writing a thesis on encryption and had a personal interest in cryptography, so he figured it would be a fun experiment to purchase a few. It didn't seem like much to spend 150 kroner, worth about $26, on some 5,600 bitcoins.[2] As the months went by, he forgot about the whole thing. It wasn't until Bitcoin began to receive widespread attention from journalists in April 2013 that he remembered his tiny gamble. Although he had forgotten his digital wallet's password, he gave it a few tries, got back into his account, and came to a stark realization: His $26 bet had ballooned into $886,000. He took a fifth of his collection and used it as down payment to buy himself a flat in Oslo's trendy and expensive Tøyen neighborhood.

The Bitcoin *nouveau riche* don't go it alone. Naturally, they seek legal advice and representation. There's a growing class of attorneys who do just that—and yes, they bill in bitcoins. Ryan Hurley is a lawyer in Scottsdale, Arizona, whose expertise is innovation: renewable energy, water laws, and medical marijuana. Digital money fit right in. Banks have traditionally turned their backs on businesses in the legal marijuana industry, so those entrepreneurs had an interest in nonbank money like bitcoins. Hurley looked into the matter and soon ended up with a Bitcoin millionaire client of his own, one who needed legal advice on starting a new Bitcoin mining business. Most of them are like that, Hurley told me. They struck virtual gold, and now they want to reinvest the proceeds in something more substantial. There's a certain degree of philosophical consistency in accepting bitcoins as payment from these folks, so Hurley convinced his colleagues it was a good idea. But Bitcoin's wild price fluctuations made the firm's managing partner, Jordan Rose, uneasy. She had a condition: Cash them out for paper money every 24 hours. She wasn't alone in her reasoning. Halfway across the world, the Winheller law firm in Germany does the same thing. The firm made a calculated decision to accept bitcoins as payment to draw clients from that industry, and it worked. The firm represents the owners of online exchanges in Germany and South America, an entrepreneur who commands a pool of miners and the maker of a Bitcoin ATM. But an attorney at the firm, Lutz Auffenberg, said the capriciousness of daily Bitcoin prices is too much for the firm to handle. "You can pay in bitcoins. But we do not keep them," he told me. "Because of the volatility."

Those price swings are why most businesses that want to take bitcoins are frightened off. On any given day, the price of a bitcoin could swing $10 in either direction. That doesn't make it very easy to plan ahead, which is an absolute necessity. I spent two years writing about U.S. small businesses for CNNMoney, and if there's anything I learned talking to a few thousand entrepreneurs, it's that the ability to plan ahead is sacrosanct. Revenue, costs, taxes—everything needs to be steady and dependable. Lucky for them, merchant-friendly services like the international digital wallet company Coinbase have popped up. The San Francisco company charges a slim 1 percent to convert your earned bitcoins into local currency (after the first $1 million, which is free). That means businesses that don't want to ever expose themselves to Bitcoin volatility can use Coinbase to accept bitcoins and change them into dollars on a daily basis. This has opened the door for all kinds of businesses.

You'd think Subway is as corporate as it gets. There are more than 41,000 restaurants in more than 100 countries, and rest assured, they all emit that bread exhaust smell we Americans know so well. Whether the signs are in English, Arabic, or Russian, the logo and design are instantly recognizable. But it's not as cookie-cutter as it seems. These are individually owned franchises, and entrepreneurs are free to experiment a bit. In Japan, there's a whole lot of fish in their sandwich menus. The company's corporate executives tell me you can get a mean lamb sub in Southeast Asia that's finger-lickin' good. And in Allentown, Pennsylvania, a cheery young MBA student is trying out electronic money. Sapan Shah is accepting bitcoins at his Subway franchise. He was 23 years old when I interviewed him in late 2013, and he was three weeks into it. It's totally weird and unprecedented, but it seemed like an innovative, fun thing to do. A $5 foot-long went for something like 0.006 BTC, an awkward total that doesn't lend itself too well to a commercial jingle. But customers didn't mind, and neither did Shah. To his surprise, it took off overnight. Some folks told him they traveled hundreds of miles just for the opportunity to bite into a real-life sandwich bought with invisible money. The move ended up being a positive attention-grabber of its own.

The transaction is painless and relatively simple. After an employee makes the sandwich, Shah rings up the order on a computer tablet. An app on the tablet automatically checks the prevailing price of a bitcoin and converts the dollar price into bitcoins. The app generates a black-and-white image on the tablet screen (called a QR code). Instead of pulling out a wallet, a customer reaches for her phone and scans the image. Presto.

The right amount of bitcoins gets sent to Shah's account and the transaction is done. Shah converts them to dollars once a week so he can pay his bills. "We can't pay our rent in Bitcoin," he told me.

Subway franchise owner Sapan Shah prepares a sandwich at his shop.

At about the same time that Subway was dabbling with digital money, on the opposite end of the country, Josh Arias was just getting the hang of it. A tech-savvy customer had recently walked into his barbershop and asked if he could pay in bitcoins. Arias thought it wouldn't hurt, so he accepted what was then a fraction of a bitcoin worth about $30. Jay Yerxa kept coming back and paying in bitcoins, and Arias kept taking them. He warmed up to the idea over time, realizing how much money he could save by lowering transaction costs. Arias could avoid the stiff merchant fees when customers swipe their credit cards, which usually cost 2.75 percent or more of every transaction. By comparison, Coinbase only skimmed 1 percent off every haircut. It doesn't sound like much, but for an entrepreneur, these numbers can mean the difference between keeping an establishment in tip-top shape and letting it slowly fall apart. Small businesses typically operate on razor-thin profit margins. Saving that 1 or 2 percent adds up over the course of a year. Arias also enjoyed how smooth the process is: A customer pulls out a smartphone, and the deal is done in a flash. No need to count cash or a trip to the register.

"The transaction speed is huge for me. I can accept it in seconds," he said.

More importantly, though, unlike the risk-averse attorneys who cash out their bitcoins the first chance they get, Arias embraces the rolling tide of market prices. That 0.2457 BTC he received for that first haircut quadrupled in value to $110 a few months later. Not bad for a single customer.

Reno barber Josh Arias

"The way it's going right now, I definitely want everyone paying in bitcoins," he said over the phone. "It's a gamble. It has its ups and downs, but there have been more ups than downs."

If it weren't for that one Bitcoin enthusiast customer, Arias might not have ever thought about taking the plunge. And that's how it usually works. Customers start asking if they can pay in bitcoins, and business owners are forced to consider it. One fellow in Australia told me he thinks of himself as a Bitcoin evangelist, because he never buys from a local shop without first pestering them about accepting bitcoins. Business owners all across the world have told me the same. And, not surprisingly, it's what led CheapAir.com to become the first-ever business to allow customers to book flights with bitcoins.

Sometime in 2013, someone asked a customer service representative at the Los Angeles company whether the website would accept cryptocurrency as payment. Clueless as to what in the world the person was talking about, the travel advisor passed the question along to bosses. The email eventually made its way to CEO Jeff Klee, who remembered reading about Bitcoin some months back. Klee thought the company might position itself as more forward-thinking and tap into a new market if they were the first to do it, so he gave the go-ahead. They started accepting them on November 21, 2013, and within a week, the company had received $6,800 worth of Bitcoin orders. That's nothing when you consider the website sells $160 million in airline tickets a year, but it was still more than Klee was expecting. And there was something else. This new option offered a chance for Klee to reduce his exposure to credit card chargebacks. Most customers don't think about it, but the same safety feature that protects you from fraudulent businesses and lets you cancel credit card charges is a total pain for small business owners. When someone steals your credit card and racks up charges at a place like CheapAir.com, Klee gets stuck with the bill. On the other hand, Bitcoin transactions are final, so deals are worry-free for Klee.

"Credit card fraud is a huge problem for us," Klee said. "There's so many people out there using stolen credit cards. The process we have to go through to screen transactions that could be fraud requires human labor to research. It's very expensive for us to figure out if it is a legitimate sale or not. With Bitcoin, we don't have that risk."

I asked him why anyone would want to buy a flight with bitcoins. Was it the highly private nature of digital currency? Klee explained that couldn't be it, because government travel regulations require him to still ask for every customer's identity. He thinks it's just the ease of purchase. A few clicks on a computer—copy your digital wallet address, paste it—and you're through. There's no need to pull out a credit card and type in 22-plus digits. Judging by the number of customers taking that option, Klee said the move was a hit.

"I think this is the kind of thing that'll gain more momentum over time. As more companies accept Bitcoin, it will snowball. If you can buy more things with Bitcoin and it gains critical mass, it'll grow exponentially," he said.

Within weeks of my conversation with Klee, Overstock.com announced it too would start accepting bitcoins. It was a momentous occasion. You could now buy everything from futons to footwear in bitcoins. It was a major bet for Overstock.com, a publicly traded company that Wall Street values at $378 million. The idea to accept bitcoins played right into CEO Patrick Byrne's Libertarian ideals. He projected the company might receive $5 million in bitcoins in a year's time. He was wrong. It was an underestimate. The company raked in $1 million in bitcoins in the first two months. Customers were using the cryptocurrency to buy bed sheets, cell phone accessories, appliances, computers, and much more.[3] The world started taking this weird electronic money more seriously.[4]

Back at that Subway shop in Pennsylvania, Shah no longer seemed like such an oddball.

It's not like every shop will take your bitcoins, though. The electronic money is useless in nearly every store you can think of. I have yet to walk into any clothing retailer, restaurant, movie theater, coffee shop, or supermarket that accepts them. Anytime I mention it, employees behind the cash register just give me a weird stare.

But true Bitcoin enthusiasts are hackers to the core, life hacks included. Alex Krusz fits the bill. He's a web developer in Somerville, Massachusetts, who figured out a way to use them anywhere. It all relies on a specific gift card system. Gyft is a digital gift card that you can manage with your smartphone. It's a smart company backed by Google Ventures and several other groups of rich entrepreneurs. The service lets you upload your existing physical gift cards to your phone, buy new ones, send them to friends and use them right on the spot. If it functions smoothly, you'll never need plastic again. Here's the pivotal detail: Gyft accepts bitcoins as payment. So, when Krusz shops at Whole Foods, he opens up the Gyft app on his phone, uses bitcoins to purchase a $100 Whole Foods gift card, and uses the gift card to buy his groceries.

Sure, it takes an extra step and defeats the whole purpose of efficient, digital transactions. And it's worth noting Krusz doesn't really buy his high-priced, organic snacks with bitcoins. It's technically a gift card loaded with U.S. dollars. But with little effort, he does manage to quickly convert bitcoins into food.

That by itself should defeat any questions about whether bitcoins have actual value. Using this neat trick, you can get by on just bitcoins with little extra effort. Using the Gyft system should work at any major retailer, because the company has deals with more than 200 of them, including CVS, Target, and Victoria's Secret.

Then there are those who don't want to spend their bitcoins at all. To them, this digital contraption is more commodity than currency. These are the speculative investors who are drawn in by the prospect that the value of Bitcoin might be in for another explosive takeoff. After all, the price of a single bitcoin went from $12 to $1,131 between late 2012 and 2013. You might as well have been an early stage investor in Facebook, Instagram, or WhatsApp. A few months' savings could have made you a millionaire.

David Rabahy is a 55-year-old software consultant in Northville, Michigan, who is doing what anyone his age should: planning for retirement. In 2013 he decided to make bitcoins part of his portfolio, so he spent $10,000 buying them from several online exchanges. He also moved $25,000 out of his Roth IRA with Fidelity and into SecondMarket's Bitcoin Investment Trust. The combined funds briefly ballooned in value and topped out at more than $100,000 during the peak in late 2013—before falling to about half that. But Rabahy doesn't mind. He plans to ride the market for a while.

"I feel fantastic," he said. "I'm not in it for the quick buck. I'm not selling at $400 or $500 or $600. I believe in this the way Edison believed in electricity. This is a fundamental technology for the ages. I'm in it for the long haul."

To Rabahy, this is about principle. It irked him to see the U.S. government bail out failed Wall Street institutions and pick winners and losers. By contrast, no government has considered offering financial assistance to any of the many collapsed Bitcoin exchanges, like Mt.Gox. While that makes it more of a risky investment than, say, AIG or Goldman Sachs, Rabahy said those firms represent everything he opposes.

"Bitcoin is a true unadulterated open market. I couldn't ignore it," he said. "It's in line with my personal beliefs. People, individuals, companies all have to be responsible. If you are responsible and you take care of business, you'll earn the success that you get. If you're irresponsible, you'll suffer the consequences."

He isn't the only one nearing retirement with a hefty stake in a highly speculative investment. Halfway across the globe in Perth, Australia, is 60-year-old Mike Wallace. He's a former IT guy who worked at his country's largest telecom and had accrued nearly $1 million worth of real estate and stocks. But he was open to something a little more risky. That's when a TV piece about Bitcoin popped up on the news.

"It was love at first sight for me," he recalled. "I'd never even heard of it. I'd kept away from electronic currencies in the past, because they all didn't look like they had legs to me. But when I heard the word 'Bitcoin,' it just struck a chord with me. I went straight to Google and that night transferred money straight to Mt.Gox."

He sunk $15,000 into 150 bitcoins. He's seen that investment rise from $15,000 to $150,000, then fall back down to $67,210. He doesn't mind the erratic pricing, because that's exactly what this portion of his savings is for.

"It's part of the extreme speculative part of my portfolio," he said. "You've got to have some real estate, stocks, cash, and balance that among asset classes. This provides me a new asset class that is not correlated with any of the other asset classes. If the dollar goes up, gold does down. Oil goes up, dollar goes down. But with Bitcoin, there's no particular correlation so far."

It struck me as odd that he'd spend so much on a whim, so I asked Wallace what his wife and two daughters think about it.

"They're not really particularly interested," he said. "To them, it's just one of Dad's crazy things."

―――――――――――

The most recent entrants into the Bitcoin world are professional money, wealthy Silicon Valley types who sit on tons of cash and like to think they can recognize a great idea when they see one. Because if you invest $1 million into the right company today, that might lead to cashing out $1 billion when the company goes public or gets bought out by a giant competitor. They take all kinds of approaches: investing in Bitcoin-related companies, starting bitcoin-collecting investment funds, and buying up bunches of bitcoins themselves.

Marc Andreessen's strategy is to get behind companies that deal with bitcoins, but he has said he doesn't own too many bitcoins himself.[5] Keep in mind that this is the entrepreneur who helped start Netscape, maker of one of the world's first Web browsers. In 2011 he was named CNET's most influential investor, having placed huge bets on companies like Twitter and Skype when they were still startups. He's a powerful investor with superstar status, so people were listening in early 2014, when he compared the value of Bitcoin's technological innovation to personal computers in 1975 and the Internet in 1993. By then, his venture capital firm, Andreessen Horowitz, had invested nearly $50 million in Bitcoin-related startups and announced it was still searching for investing opportunities. One of those was Ripple, a small group of computer programmers that, inspired by Bitcoin's approach to processing payments, developed their own Internet protocol for making financial transactions.

Semi-celebrity investors Cameron and Tyler Winklevoss are taking a more Wall Street approach. The twin brothers, who are best known for their legal battle over the creation of Facebook, have created a Bitcoin-related investment fund. According to documents filed with the Security and Exchange Commission, they're in the process of launching a Winklevoss Bitcoin Trust, which will buy up bitcoins and allow investors to buy shares in the trust.[6] It's essentially a way for everyday investors to bet on the price of bitcoins without ever having to own a bitcoin. But someone else has beaten them to the punch.

That someone would be Barry Silbert, an entrepreneur who specializes in creating ways for investors to trade things that most people don't typically think can be bought or sold, such as bankruptcy claims and private company stock. His company, SecondMarket, moved into bitcoins early on and bought nearly 19,000 of them. It started a fund and drew in another 140 Bitcoin investors into the pool. The result is something called the Bitcoin Investment Trust, which is made up of about 100,000 bitcoins. That fund is slated to make its public debut in late 2014, when everyday investors with a brokerage account, like TD Ameritrade, can move money into it by buying up shares worth about 0.1 BTC each from its current investors. Sitting down with me over coffee in New York, Silbert compared his creation to the SPDR Gold Shares exchange-traded fund.

"The SPDR Gold ETF made investing in gold possible," Silbert told me. "The Bitcoin Investment Trust will look and feel just like that."

Silbert told me he moved $50,000 of his own savings into the fund—and that's apart from the $200,000 he has sunk into buying bitcoins on his own. His company also has plans to launch a digital currency exchange that will trade in all sorts of alternative virtual money, so if the price of a bitcoin rises, he wins. If it falls and some other virtual currency rises, he still wins. I asked him what happens if this all collapses.

"If the price if Bitcoin goes away, to zero, and nothing else emerges to take its place, this will be a big loss. This will be a big hole," he said. "But look, I'm an entrepreneur. You take risks, and I think it's a smart, calculated risk."

So far, we've covered people who mine bitcoins, accept them as payment, shop with them, and invest them. But what about the actual process of buying a bitcoin? It's not very easy—or fast either. Bitcoins aren't a manufactured product you can just buy off the shelf. They're actively traded on something that very closely resembles a stock market, so you have to buy them from someone else. There are three ways to do this.

Buy it from someone you know in person: This is the easiest way to do it, because you can pay in cash and seal the deal immediately. However, the Bitcoin community is still so small, there's a slim chance you'll find someone who owns any—and is willing to sell some. I wouldn't advise meeting random strangers you locate online. It's dangerous and just plain stupid. The safest approach might be to announce it on a social media platform like Facebook or Twitter and meet with an acquaintance or friend. The key is to exercise caution. Deals made this way are in cash, and if you're planning to buy an entire bitcoin or two, that could mean stuffing hundreds of dollars into your pocket.

Buy it from an online exchange: There are several to choose from, and they're all over the world. Two large American exchanges with decent reputations are Kraken.com, located in

San Francisco, and CampBX.com, located just north of Atlanta. There are many others based outside of the United States, such as the large Slovenian operation Bitstamp.net. But be patient— and on your guard. You'll be sending money to an entity you'll never meet in person.

For starters, this isn't the way to go if you want to acquire a bitcoin in a day or two. These websites have a lengthy registration process that's a bit like opening a bank account. Keep in mind, that's essentially what it is. You're opening a trading account, so these companies are doing their due diligence to abide by government know-your-customer rules and anti– money laundering laws.

For example, Kraken first requires you to get verified, which means submitting a government-issued ID, address, proof of residence (like a utility bill), Social Security number, phone number, and date of birth. Bitstamp demands an identical procedure before you can start trading on the site. CampBX lets you trade up to $1,000 a day with minimal personal information, but it requires more if you plan to withdraw more than that in a single day.

As for loading up funds into your account, that's an extensive process too. To get money into Bitstamp, most people will have to wire money through an international bank transfer, which takes two to five business days. CampBX asks for mailed money orders, which can take up to two weeks.

Then there's the fact that lots of exchanges are sketchy fly-by-night operations that reveal little information about themselves, such as where they're located or who runs them. Imagine if you were dealing with a bank and had no idea who owned it or where it was headquartered. It's that shady. One example is BTC-e.com, which despite its aloofness, remains one of the world's top destinations for trading bitcoins online.

Search results on Google say the exchange is based in Bulgaria, but the website itself states it is governed by laws in Cyprus. Site owners have declined to identify themselves in the past and dodge questions about how and where they operate. Even trusted operations that have been open for years and traded millions of dollars in bitcoins, such as Tokyo's Mt.Gox (mtgox. com), have fizzled out in the past. But this is the most popular way to get into the Bitcoin game. Once you're in, trading is relatively easy. Just don't expect to start quickly.

Once you're set up, acquiring bitcoins on an exchange is similar to buying commodities like gold or silver on a trading floor. Sellers place sell orders, known as "asks," at the price at which they're willing to let go of a bitcoin. Buyers place buy orders, known as "bids," at the price they're willing to pay. The exchange matches a seller with a buyer so they can conduct the deal.

But keep one thing in mind. Nakamoto specifically designed Bitcoin as a trustless system meant to get rid of third parties— and that's exactly what online exchanges are. Once you send them your money, there's no true guarantee you'll ever get it back. The tale of Mt.Gox, which is told later in this book, explains this at length.

Buy it from a Bitcoin ATM: For most of the world, this isn't an option yet, but several entrepreneurs are working on it. Given that bitcoins are virtual, not physical, these won't spit out metal coins. They're actually just computers that take your money and send your bitcoins to a digital wallet.

A few are already popping up around the world, but it will be a while before they catch on in the United States. Manufacturers are trying to secure legal permission to set them up, and nearly every state requires special money services business licenses, so it's an uphill climb. That's why San Diego–based

Genesis Coin is setting up machines outside the U.S., north and south of the borders. The company president, Evan Rose, struck deals to place Bitcoin ATMs in Tijuana, Mexico, as well as Quebec City and Whistler in Canada. Another company is Lamassu, which is based in the British Virgin Islands and manufactures out of Portugal. It already has dozens of working machines in Australia, Finland, and Slovakia, but CEO Zach Harvey told me he's trying hard to expand in the United States. He's attempting to fill a giant void.

"If you wanted to get a bitcoin today—in one day—without meeting a stranger, there is no solution," Harvey told me.

Except I'm in New York, where there's a fascinating group that meets every Monday to do just that.

The violent jerks of the cab ride had my stomach turned into a knot. I did my best to pay attention to Charlie Payne, my CNNMoney pal sitting in the back seat with me, but the momentum from the sudden pushes and tugs made it damn near impossible. I tried to peer around the driver's seat to recalibrate and catch a glimpse of the road ahead as we made our way south into New York's Financial District. Now would be a terrible time to puke, I muttered under my breath. We were just a few minutes away from actually seeing some Bitcoin action in person.

That's the thing about a network and a currency that's driven entirely by intricate computer calculations. It's all about empowering individuals, but there's rarely a human around.

This Monday evening was to be my initial trip to New York City's Bitcoin Center. The one-of-a-kind place where Bitcoin enthusiasts could buy and sell their tokens on something that was supposed to resemble a trading floor was appropriately located at the southern tip of Manhattan, next to all the banks and financial institutions this tiny little currency was meant to overturn. We stopped at Wall Street, popped the trunk, and lifted the camera gear.

It was 6:30, just over two hours past the stock market closing time, so the sea of suits that would normally flood these shaded cobblestone streets had cleared out. Now it was just a few tourists here and there. I noted how empty it looked.

We took a right on Broad Street. I couldn't help but stare in awe at the massive, gray columns and elaborate façade of the New York Stock Exchange—home to 2,800 listed companies valued at $18 trillion. And as the listing place for AIG, Bank of America, and Goldman Sachs stock, ground zero for the recent financial crisis. Our destination was just past the towering NYSE structure—across the street and one building over—marked by a tiny, friendly Bitcoin banner flapping in the chilly wind.

Charlie and I pulled on the glass door and walked into the tiny, dressed-down lobby. With the gray cement floor and high ceiling, it looked half-warehouse, half-nightclub. We were greeted by a small staff of smiling volunteers, and one handed me a paper badge I hung around my neck. "HAK Hackathon 9034," it read. I introduced myself, and in no time a small, energetic man rounded the corner and stuck out his hand. The center's spokesman, no doubt.

"Hi! I'm James Barcia. You won't be needing that," he said, pulling the badge over my head. I pulled it back down.

"Actually, I'd like to buy a bitcoin today," I said. He gave me a surprised look. If I was serious about that, I could do that once I stepped inside, he explained. It seemed he'd seen few reporters willing to experiment firsthand.

I asked if I could start recording the conversation, and he agreed. I placed my iPhone beneath my notepad to not hold it awkwardly between us. I hoped the murmur of the crowd inside wouldn't drown out his voice.

Right off the bat, Barcia started listing an odd series of disclaimers. "It is not a trading floor, it's not a brokerage, it's not a clearinghouse. What we are at this stage is an information center, built around Bitcoin advocacy. We try to grow the audience for Bitcoin through Bitcoin 101 classes, which are free and open to the public. We take walk-ins. We're open 10:00 AM to 10:00 PM, seven days a week."

"There's really no sales going on here unless it's an individual person-to-person sale," he said.

From somewhere inside, I heard a man yell at the top of his lungs, "Five-ninety bid, at six hundred!"

Barcia smiled. "When I said we're not a trading floor, it means we're not an intermediary. We don't take a commission of any kind. Everything's free down to the open bar that we have. Because what we want is people to see the technology in use, so for that, we provide a little theater, a little bit of hospitality."

Without a meeting place like this, Barcia explained, Bitcoin enthusiasts all over the city would scramble to meet at a Starbucks here, a Whole Foods there. All the center does is round them up, and more than 100 show up every Monday night. For newcomers to better understand the buying and selling process, the center recreates the scene of a classic stock exchange floor, like the big NYSE guys next door. But by "recreate," I mean actually do it. There are clerks—"mock clerks," Barcia stressed—taking orders from traders. And the yeller? That's the center's auctioneer—that is, "mock auctioneer." If they didn't have it this way, it would just be a quiet room with people whispering and snapping pictures of each other's smartphones to swap QR codes and initiate transfers.

I raised an eyebrow. "So it's not a trading floor, but there is trading going on—on that floor."

"Yes. It's other people trading in our space," Barcia responded.

Another yell from the back: "Five-ninety bid, at six hundred ask!"

Barcia continued: "It would not be easy to understand how to transact using this technology if you didn't hear or see something."

That seemed fair. I asked him to guide me through the right manners of approaching someone to buy a bitcoin.

"But again, it's very hands off," he reminded me as we walked. "To facilitate in any substantive way is probably going to be not in line with the regulations. Given that there's no regulations, we're being extra safe."

Barcia led us into the sparsely crowded, dimly lit room. The nightclub-like glow came from the high ceiling's neon blue beams, which fanned out like large tines on a leaf rake. A semicircle of fold-out tables had been positioned to corral two dozen young men and women in the center of the room. On one wall, a white projector screen tallied the deals of the night. I couldn't make out all the numbers, but it looked like bitcoins were going for $600 a pop.

At the edge of the pit, a bearded man in a suit and orange bowtie stood on a soap box, glancing at the paper in his left hand and yelling the auction prices. He was the trading floor squawker, as they say in finance.

"Fiiiive-ninety! We've got fiiiive-ninety! Five-ninety bid, at six hundred ask!" he shouted with a grin. He seemed like he was having fun.

Meanwhile, several young men with orange shirts draped over their dress wear wormed their way through the crowd, jotting down notes and scurrying back and forth between buyers and sellers. We passed them. An imposing man in a bright bowtie waited for us in the back, introducing himself as Nick Spanos, one of the center's founders. Charlie and I walked him up a flight of stairs, allowing us to look down at the crowd below.

"A year or two from now we'll be trading pork bellies for bitcoins hopefully," he said. "We want to be the first regulated exchange in the spirit of the New York Stock Exchange. Everything they do next door, we want to do over here."

I found it odd to compare the NYSE, which easily trades $30 billion a day, to a half-empty room of Libertarians and computer programmers. "But the New York Stock Exchange is trading with known companies that have commodities and assets that we're familiar with, trading in dollars, a currency that's been proven over the last few hundred years," I responded.

Yes, but the block chain's innovative design will win people over when they recognize its revolutionary potential outside of finance, he told me.

"The guy who invented the wheel loved it because it rolled," Spanos said. "He didn't know it was going to be sending jumbo jets into the sky. He didn't know that...everything was going to be invented around his wheel: clocks, machinery, and stuff like that. That's where we're at with the use of Bitcoin so far. Bitcoin will change the world. People are looking at it and trying to fit it in a box in their brain; they're trying to associate it with something they already know. It's never existed before."

Spanos pointed into the crowd. "There's Goldman Sachs guys in there. They won't tell you. But there's Goldman Sachs guys looking to buy a thousand bitcoins...a lot of them said they're going to be working for us soon."

We wrapped up our interview, and I walked downstairs to hunt for someone willing to sell me a bitcoin. I approached the bartender behind a foldout table and asked her for advice. She introduced herself as Mira from Russia and offered to help.

"You have an Android?"

I pulled out my iPhone. She smirked. This is going to be a little complicated then, she sighed.

I thought I had already done my homework. I had just created a Bitcoin wallet earlier in the day at the office. It was an easy process, no longer than 10 minutes. I just logged on to Bitcoin.org, downloaded the third-party program MultiBit, and figured this would be a cinch, I told her.

Except that I did it on my laptop, she corrected me. And without my laptop, I couldn't access that wallet. I'd have to open a new digital wallet on my smartphone. The problem is, at the time, Apple had flexed its muscle and purged every Bitcoin wallet from its App Store. I'd have to run this all through the Internet browser.

Mira directed me to Coinbase.com, and I started a new account in under a minute. But I couldn't maneuver the site. She suggested Blockchain.info instead, and that worked fine. The site gave me a wallet address and showed a zero balance. She cheered, and I raised my glass in celebration.

"Do I really have to give someone this address?" I asked, pointing to a long string that made my eyes glaze over: *162GDziX-pMVd9afauFX3xLFWwNWgiYDHxf*. It sure seemed inefficient.

Mira laughed, took my phone, and scrolled down, pointing me to the QR code, a block of black pixels that doubled as my address. Just have them take a picture of this, she said.

I approached a clerk—sorry, mock clerk—and asked what the going rate was. He told me the folks in the room were selling at $600, and buyers were currently paying $590. I pulled out my phone and checked Preev.com, a site that averages the rate at three large online exchanges.

"It's going for $580 online," I said before realizing what was going on. "Ah, but I guess there's a premium for buying it now in cash?"

He nodded. "You'd have to wait a few days to set up a bank account on an exchange. Here, you get it right away."

So then, $590. The price hadn't budged all night, the clerk told me. But with Charlie lugging around heavy camera equipment, I didn't want to keep him waiting. I told him I'd be willing to do $595.

"That'll put you at the front of the line," he said, and darted off. A few minutes later, the auctioneer started yelling my bid. It didn't seem to get anyone's attention. Then a cheery fellow wearing a straw trilby hat—and what looked like a blue lab coat—walked over. He was clearly experienced—a fast talker who breezed through the details and never batted an eye. He saw the lost look on my face and slowed down, kindly walking me through the deal.

We'd negotiate, I'd give him my address, and hand him the cash. "We're gentlemen here, so I'll send you the bitcoin first," he said.

His name was Mark Anthony, and he'd been doing this for years as a trader at the New York Cotton Exchange, then later on the floor of the American Stock Exchange. With his pen, he lifted the paper hanging from his pocket and revealed the embroidered logo on his blue coat.

"I was one of those, like a lot of people, I kind of discounted the idea of Bitcoin. I'm an investment guy now," he said.

So we negotiated. He said $600, I bumped to $596, and we met at $597. We whipped out our smartphones, and he snapped a picture of the QR code on my screen. A minute later, I refreshed the webpage and saw a 1 BTC balance. I reached into my corduroy suit pocket, but he motioned for me to wait, and with a finger, flicked back the narrow-brim of his hat. The transfer hadn't been verified yet, he explained. It wasn't yet official until the computers hooked up to the Bitcoin network could chime in, which would take just a few minutes. Sure enough, in four minutes, a tiny number "1" popped up on his screen, next to our listed transaction. We were charged a 6¢ transaction fee by the computer network of miners, and now it was official.

I handed him a wad of $20 bills, and Anthony called me an amateur for not paying in higher denominations. We shook hands.

"Good transaction," he said. "And now you can see how fast it was. It was frictionless, and the cost of the transaction was a whopping six cents."

The CNNMoney newsroom was now the proud owner of a Bitcoin. What a rush. Cutting that deal was a blast, and I got the sense that I had taken part in something special, brushed against something truly innovative. But as I exited the building and walked onto Broad Street, now dark beneath a cloudy night sky, the excitement wore off. My enthusiasm got replaced by a pit in my stomach. Did I just spend $597 on a sham?

CHAPTER 5

But Is It Money?

IT'S EASY to call Bitcoin "funny money." Judging by today's standards, it's nothing short of ridiculous. You can't stuff them into your wallet, because they don't physically exist. No one has ever seen a bitcoin. The metal coins pictured in news stories are little more than novelty items. The real thing is nothing but ones and zeros. The closest you'll get to seeing a bitcoin is staring at a few numerical digits on a computer screen. To top it all off, they're never technically in your possession. All you get is a digital wallet that lays a claim to something that exists on the block chain.

It's evanescent, intangible—a digital ghost.

But it satisfies the three-prong definition of money.[1] People are willing to pay in government-issued cash to get one, so it's clearly a store of value (albeit a shaky one). Thousands of merchants and websites accept them as payment and price their goods in bitcoins, so it's a unit of account. And in those circles, whenever they're used, it's a medium of exchange.

Most people still get a knot in their stomach about the whole idea, though. The virtual world might cut it for storing our songs and movies, but our hard-earned cash? No way. The idea of independent, electronic moola just doesn't square with the modern concept of the stuff: government-backed, printed bills. Who can blame them? That's the only form of it we know from personal experience. Everyone in the modern world uses paper currency. That's why it's easy to take the concept of money for granted. It's always with us and constantly in the same form. But as with most things, it's a matter of perspective. A Chinese proverb is instructive here: "The fish is the last to know water."

Who in 2014 doubts the purchasing power of a U.S. dollar? It's backed by nothing but the faith that the U.S. government will make good on its debt. Yet Venezuelans under their country's oppressive socialist regime are still clamoring for those green U.S. Federal Reserve notes.[2] Once upon a time, though, gold and silver reigned supreme, and paper bills were seen as a ludicrous plaything.

If we take a step back and examine our history with money, a curious pattern emerges. Money is always changing form, evolving right alongside us. It's just like government and art, a reflection of who we are at the time. When we were simple and barbaric, so was money. As we developed complex business practices, money got complicated too. Books and movies rarely give it a second thought and merely treat it as background material, showing money as if it had always been paper bills and coins. But it has a bizarre history. There have been times when finance was conducted with sticks—even in Britain as late as the American Revolutionary War. A great place to start is a century ago on the Pacific island of Yap, where a few natives in grass skirts taught European economists a thing or two about money.

The year was 1903, and the young American anthropologist William Henry Furness III traveled to Yap, a lonely speck in the middle of the Pacific some 800 miles north of New Guinea.[3] Germany had a small outpost there, which allowed him to mingle with the secluded tribe. To his surprise, this tiny society of a few thousand islanders had developed a full-blown, complex financial system. In the absence of precious metal, the natives relied on a strange form of coinage: massive, stone wheels. These *fei*, as they were called, looked like flat, rocky donuts. Value was judged by the quality and size of the stone, which sometimes ranged up to 12 feet in diameter. The downside was obvious. These weren't exactly the kind of thing you could carry around for casual trading up and down the rolling green hills of Yap's dense forest. On the other hand, stealing your neighbor's *fei* was, in some cases, downright impossible. Immovable currency gave birth to an unprecedented form of exchange. If a deal involved so much money that it required moving an extremely heavy *fei*, both sides would just agree that a transfer of ownership took place. The islanders were past the crude notion of expecting someone to physically possess a stone to signify wealth. The community generally acknowledged who owned what. In fact, one village recognized a certain family's massive wealth, even though no one had actually seen their *fei*. There was no use in punishing the family for its misfortune: Their giant stone was lost at sea during a storm as it made its way there from another island. The lesson from Yap for economists at the turn of the 20th century was something of a reminder: Money can be anything, as long as people have faith that it works.

Former World Bank official Felix Martin uses the example of Yap to illustrate a pivotal point in his book, *Money: The Unauthorized Biography*. Don't mistake currency for money. Those giant rocks were the Yap islanders' form of currency. Their money consisted of something deeper and harder to see.

"Yap's money was not the *fei*, but the underlying system of credit accounts and clearing of which they helped to keep track," he wrote.

An eight-foot-high Yap fei in the village of Gachpar

The method for keeping track of ownership—and who owes what—that's the key part of money we often overlook. Sometimes that's invisible, and it often takes a form that's different than what we're used to today.

For instance, take the first-known record of an accounting system. In the ancient Mesopotamian city of Uruk around 3100 BCE, the Sumerians began carving symbols into tablets to represent ownership, such as receipt of grain.[4] Fast forward to about 1650 BCE and travel a few hundred miles up the Euphrates River to the Babylonian town of Sippar. A clay tablet found there was inscribed with this promise: At harvest time, someone named Amil-mirra would pay 330 measures of barley to whomever held that tablet.[5] Receipts were issued whenever someone deposited grain at a temple or palace. Harvard University professor Niall Ferguson has noted the fact that they would "pay the bearer" instead of a specific named person shows that debts were transferable—evidence of a lending system that was complex and robust. There was no Babylonian Federal Credit Union, but at least there was a mechanism you could trade with and pass along wealth.

Move forward another millennium, sometime around the fifth or sixth century BCE. We're in Lydia, an Iron Age kingdom in what would later be western Turkey. This is what archeologists say is the most likely birthplace of the metal coin.[6] The concept was so new and effective, coinage soon caught on in nearby Persia and Greece. It was a major achievement. Lugging around bearer bond tablets became a thing of the past. This new, metal-based system of account could be used to close any kind of deal, because it easily transferred value and was light enough to not be a chore. Of all the materials in the world, why metal? The answer is rooted in the need for a monetary unit of account to be something you can measure. Metal can easily be melted down and forged into lumps of a certain size and weight. Plus, once they've been etched, it's not easy to create fake copies. It also didn't hurt that precious metals were rare and had an alluring, brilliant shine.

When the Ancient Greeks adopted metallic coinage, they were still left with a question of how to measure it. They used *stadia* for distance and *drachmae* for weight. So the Greeks settled on calling coins "drachmas." Cities minted the coins. The silver and gold coins usually showed the head of a city-state's patron god on one side and a city symbol or name on the other. Athens, for instance, showed Athena and an owl. The whole concept, however, was so new that people at the time still experienced this social technology with fresh eyes. Because of that, their writings provide valuable perspective. From Aristotle's point of view, human beings created money merely to facilitate trade.[7] It was a human phenomenon whose only purpose was as a means of exchange. That didn't impart any inherent value in the coins themselves.

"Money seems to be a nonsense and altogether a thing of law and by nature nothing, because if its users change the currency, the original one is not worth anything," Aristotle said in his treatise, *Politics*.

Tetradrachm (4 drachma) coin used in Athens from around 410 BCE

At around this time, Ancient China also used paper bank notes that served as receipts of value stored elsewhere, much like the Mesopotamian tablets of old.[8] But more remarkable was the Jixia Academy scholars' sophisticated take on money. They saw currency—for them gold, pearls, jade—as a ruler's tool. It was an emperor's privilege, a way to monopolize control. Independent currencies were nothing short of rebellion.

Back west, though, they were still grappling with the notion that money was a manmade device. Even the Greek word for money, *nomisma*, meant "something assigned by usage or custom."[9] They recognized it wasn't natural. No god descended from the heavens and gave it value. It was a constructed social technology. And while it might not be worthless, it was in some sense, meaningless without context. Money wasn't metal. Metal represented something else.

This wisdom was lost over time. The fall of the Roman Empire provides a notable example. The Romans adopted coinage and it worked for them for centuries. Remember, it was a Roman denarius with Caesar's face that the Pharisees in the Bible showed Jesus when they asked him about taxes.[10] But metal took on a value of its own. As the ever-warring Romans were saddled with military costs, emperors thought they could get away with paying soldiers by minting more coins and simply reducing the silver content in each denarius.[11] It was a dumb move. By then, people valued the metal content itself, so silver denarii were worth less and inflation kicked in. In 301 CE, a pound of gold got you 50,000 silver denarii. Just 38 years later, a pound of gold fetched 20 million denarii. The futile attempt by government to pay debts by debasing a currency isn't new.

Those Roman coins ended up circulating for centuries. The system of metal coinage stuck around too, and kingdoms that sprouted up all over Medieval Europe eventually started issuing their own. Similar to the Chinese take on currency, minting was a royal privilege. The actual metal in the coins became so important, though, that the region's shortage of silver became a monumental problem. Kings saw the hunt for it as essential to maintaining wealth and control, and the quest for it was deemed a noble cause. The Crusades starting in 1096 CE were partly an attempt to plunder the Muslim territories of their precious metal, as were Spain and Portugal's murderous conquistador trips to the Americas in the 1400s and beyond.[12] Yet monarchies too made the mistake of attaching a static value to metal. Spain caused its own inflationary spiral by importing massive loads of silver from a 45,000-ton mountain of it in Peru. There was also the nasty fact that royalty retained control of the mint, allowing them to get away with looting their own subjects by debasing currency. This practice, called "seigniorage" (from the French term for feudal lord, *seigneur*), didn't sit well with the noble classes who became poorer at the king's expense. It especially didn't work when kings would borrow massive amounts of money to fund wars, only to default. And who would question them? They could simply kill a detractor in the public square. But borrowing was not just for kings. As merchants became increasingly important to society, the modern practice of banking also arose to process complex, high-value transactions.[13] IOUs were issued that could be traded or inherited. Private paper money had appeared.

A turning point came in England, when an outsider from the Netherlands took the throne in 1689. The recently deceased King Charles II had just defaulted on his debts, and the new king, William of Orange, was at risk of repeating that financial mistake. That's when a Scottish trader suggested a brand new public-private venture: the Bank of England.[14] It would promise to fund the king as long as the bank could retain control of issuing money in the form of bank notes. The modern financial system was starting to take shape. It wasn't exactly progressive, however. British subjects at the time were still using a crude form of currency called tally sticks: notches of wood that would detail tax payments and could be split down the middle so that each side had a receipt.[15] But once this Paleolithic practice was done away with in 1834, what remained were precious metal coins and bank notes backed by gold and silver.

The system worked well enough that it caught on around the world. But over time, a bimetallic standard of gold and silver didn't cut it, because it caused awkward monetary problems. If a nation's silver coins were undervalued, they would be siphoned off to a place that valued them more highly, and the first country would suddenly have a silver coin shortage. Nations dropped the idea and adopted the gold standard by

1880, meaning that units of currency were fixed to a certain weight of gold.[16] It all depended on the country's stockpile of the stuff. Under this new system, prices remained stable and international trade exploded. And because paper bills could be cashed in for a specific amount of gold, governments were barred from haplessly printing money. Any devaluing of the currency would have immediate consequences. Now paper had unquestionable value, because gold had value. Aristotle's misgivings about inherent value in metal were long gone.

But governments found the gold standard unwieldy because it was so limiting. The restrictions placed on central banks meant that their hands were tied. If a country entered a recession and unemployment spiked, politicians were limited in how they could manipulate the value of currency to address national economic policy. And if someone were to find a massive gold reserve and flood the market, everyone's currency would be worth less. The world's brief flirtation with the gold standard ended in 1913 just before the outbreak of World War I as international cooperation fizzled out.[17] That was also the year the United States established its own central bank to manage monetary policy, the Federal Reserve. The repercussions were felt in no time. By the final stretch of the war in 1917, the UK inflation rate topped out at 25 percent.[18] It was the same in the United States, where inflation peaked at 18 percent in 1918.[19] But no country serves as a better example of monetary policy gone wrong than Germany.[20] The country had issued domestic war bonds it couldn't repay, and in 1923, it was overburdened by war reparation demands from the vengeful Entente Powers who had claimed victory. Everyone wanted German marks, so Germany gave them what they wanted—by printing more marks. The solution was shortsighted. Hyperinflation set in, and the country was soon printing trillion-mark bills.

The idea of gold-backed currency didn't die out all at once, though.[21] The unified system was gone, but some governments still allowed for people to cash in paper currency for gold. That was done away with during World War II, when major powers convened in Bretton Woods, New Hampshire, to come up with a new system: pegging every country's currency to the U.S. dollar.[22] It was Gold Standard Lite. As long as the U.S. kept gold reserves, other countries didn't need to. But the U.S. dollar grew so prominent that by 1971, it was clear the world had an insatiable appetite for it. President Richard Nixon ended the ability to convert dollars for gold, and the chain to gold was broken. At that moment, money everywhere became entirely fiat. It was money defined by government decree, backed by faith in government instead of metal. Its worth came from something of a self-fulfilling effect. The government mandate to use it caused people to say a currency had value, which gave it value. Now governments were totally free to maneuver their economies around—at the expense of the public at large, which has seen inflation slowly eat away at their currency's purchasing power. An issue of the *New York Times* cost 15¢ in 1970.[23] That went up to $1 in 2004 and $2.50 a decade later.

Now consider the world of today. The U.S. dollar remains the reserve currency of the world, and it's backed by nothing but the faith that the U.S. government will make good on its debt.[24] It's clear that expectation remains strong, because there's a healthy market for U.S. Treasury bills even as the national debt climbed past $17 trillion (more than the country's GDP in 2013).[25] Then what can we make of those who say the U.S. dollar is actually worthless paper because it's not backed by gold? These are the same folks who argue for a return to the gold standard citing an inherent value in gold, because it's always been money. But history shows that isn't true. Currency has been paper, gold, silver, sticks, stones, and tablets. But money has always been the system of accounts that lies beneath all of that.

Think back to the philosopher Aristotle and his realization that money is a means of exchange—there's no inherent value in whatever tool is being used to conduct that trade. But there is a requirement that supersedes all others: faith that it works, that someone else will accept it as payment too. That's why anyone in feudal England would gladly take a stick with just the right notches, and scribbles on a clay tablet would be enough to convince someone to brave bandits and lions in the Mesopotamian desert. It's why the Knights of Malta, facing a gold and silver shortage during a war in 1565, stamped *Non Aes, sed Fides* on their copper coins: "Not the metal, but trust."[26] It's a technological innovation, a means to an end.

The question now facing the world, which has moved into the age of computers and virtual networks, is whether we are willing to take money along with us into that realm. By presenting an entirely automated and digital form of currency, Bitcoin is the first revolutionary advancement in that direction. It has features that could be the next stage in the evolution of money. It might even be the first iteration of that next money. The stakes are high. There's no telling how exactly it's going to work, and the process of trial and error will mean some people's savings will be wiped out. Some might see this challenge as contrived and forced. Doesn't money work for us already? Isn't the current system of banking good enough? Prepare to be disappointed.

CHAPTER 6

The Case for Bitcoin

Banking the Unbanked

Ding. The elevator doors slid open, and all of us inside the crowded box stood still. We had nowhere to go. A mother and her children were standing right in front of us, blocking the exit. One by one, we shuffled around her. I heard some exasperated sighs, complaints about this being a routine annoyance. It wasn't until I stepped outside that I realized why we were stuck.

The line of families waiting to see clerks at the government welfare office snaked around the room several times, reaching all the way to the elevator on the far end. Babies wailed. A pregnant woman who had probably been standing for over an hour was shifting her weight uncomfortably from one foot to the other. A young man with tattoos running down his arms gave me a cold stare. We were at the Joseph Caleb Service Center in Miami's neighborhood of Brownsville, where 41 percent live below the poverty level.[1] This was the local office for the Florida Department of Children and Families' ACCESS program, which provides food, money, and medical services to those in need. This was during the worst of the recession, when nearly one in 10 Floridians were on food stamps. At the time,

I was writing for the *Miami Herald*, and I went there to see for myself how families were experiencing these troubled times. Statewide budget cuts had denied the Department of Children and Families' request to add another 150 people to help process social welfare applications. Their team of 4,500 could barely keep up with the recent flood of requests. As a result, the line inside this damp, muggy room moved at a snail's pace. I still remember that day vividly, because it showed me how slow and painful the process is of getting help to those who need it most.

Some of the folks were there for the food stamps. Others were there for the cash welfare that the federal government doles out to poor families with children. But the food stamps aren't stamps. And the cash welfare isn't cash. In both cases, the financial help comes in a plastic payment card that looks like your typical credit or debit card. It's called an Electronic Benefits Transfer card, EBT for short. It's the system adopted across the United States. For the most part, it's a great idea.

Every month or so, the government loads it up with funds, and the less fortunate of us travel to a nearby grocery store to buy what we can: breads, cereals, fruits, vegetables, meats, dairy, and seeds. Naturally, the help comes with strings attached. You can't buy tobacco, pet food, or alcohol. As for the financial help, that comes from the Temporary Assistance for Needy Families program (TANF). It isn't much—a poor family of four in Florida gets $364 a month, max—but it's sure better than nothing.[2]

However, a closer look at that TANF money actually reveals a great deal of waste. And it's not because that money gets blown on vices, like booze and casinos. It's actually because much of that money gets siphoned off by banks.

It's an issue that's plaguing the poor nationwide. It happens every time welfare recipients withdraw cash from their

EBT accounts at ATMs. They get slammed with a fee, usually around $3. If that doesn't sound like much, consider how this is experienced firsthand. Let's say you're a single parent who's barely scraping by in California, where the average welfare payment is $463 per month. The money just got loaded onto your card, and you're going to shop for school supplies at a local store that won't process small dollar debit card transactions—a routine situation. You need cash, right? So, you head to a nearby ATM and pull out enough cash for the day. Maybe that's $40. The EBT cards in California are made by Xerox, so ATM fees kick in at most banks. You just paid a 7.5 percent fee for your own money.

That very situation gets repeated several times a month, and it adds up. In California, the poor spent $19 million on ATM fees alone in 2013.[3] While that's a tiny fraction of the $3.1 billion California spent on that welfare program, it's still a massive amount of money that could have gone toward assisting another 3,419 families that year at the average rate. And for the actual families in this situation, that's money better spent on clothing or rent.

Now, there are several counterpoints to address. Why not just pull out more money and limit your trips to the ATM? It's not safe to walk around with loads of cash in your wallet, particularly if you're living in a blighted neighborhood. As for the banks, don't they have a right to charge when non-members use their services? Sure they do—even if they're profiting from the most disenfranchised of us. But that's not the point. What matters here is that a sizable portion of the population isn't a member of any bank, anywhere. That's why they're getting hit with these outrageously large surcharges.

We're not talking about some far-off place like the desert of Djibouti in Africa. No, this is going on in Detroit, Miami,

Phoenix—and just about every other metro area. In the typical large American city, more than 30 percent don't have a bank account—or leave it untouched and rely instead on extraordinarily expensive alternatives that often prey on the poor.

Patrick Murck, the attorney for the Bitcoin Foundation, was right when he warned senators in 2013 that "there is a rising tide of unbanked and underbanked people, right within our borders."

The Federal Deposit Insurance Corporation, which oversees the nation's banks, surveyed American households in 2011. It found that 17 million adults are totally unbanked. Another 51 million are "underbanked," which means that they keep a bank account somewhere, but they instead depend on expensive check cashing stores, payday loans, and pawn shops.[4] After all, when you live paycheck to paycheck, what good is a savings account? The statistics in some cities are staggering.

Metropolitan Area	Unbanked	Under-banked	Total Unbanked/ Underbanked Households
Atlanta, GA	9.7%	25.7%	*746,232*
Austin, TX	10.2%	20.4%	*185,130*
Bangor, ME	3.9%	27.1%	*19,530*
Birmingham, AL	12.1%	33%	*190,773*
Charlotte, NC	8.9%	27.8%	*272,314*
Columbus, OH	8.1%	25.3%	*239,812*
Dallas–Fort Worth, TX	9.8%	27.5%	*907,509*
Des Moines, IA	7%	23.2%	*68,856*
Detroit, MI	10.7%	19.4%	*530,362*
Houston, TX	11.9%	28.4%	*892,645*
Jacksonville, FL	6%	25%	*186,000*

Kansas City, MO/KS	10%	20.3%	*257,247*
Las Vegas, NV	6.2%	33.2%	*286,438*
Little Rock, AR	7.8%	27.8%	*117,480*
Los Angeles, CA	9.7%	18.6%	*1,231,899*
Louisville, KY	8.4%	23%	*179,294*
Memphis, TN	11.1%	16.4%	*155,925*
Miami, FL	9%	22.3%	*715,205*
New Orleans, LA	12.4%	23.2%	*180,492*
Orlando, FL	7.4%	23.5%	*244,419*
Oklahoma City, OK	9.3%	26.4%	*188,853*
Phoenix, AZ	10.6%	18.9%	*504,450*
Reno-Sparks, NV	10.9%	24.9%	*62,650*
Riverside–San Bernardino, CA	12.7%	22.3%	*484,400*
San Antonio, TX	15.5%	26%	*328,265*

Overall, more than one in four American households is in this tenuous situation. In some cities, it surpasses one in three. The causes are mixed. In the most desperate of cases, the person simply makes too little income to qualify for a bank account. Often times, it's because people just aren't financially literate. They don't realize when they're making mistakes with their money. Consider the 2006 study conducted by the University of Buffalo's School of Management, which showed that, on average, only 52 percent of high school seniors understand basic concepts about personal finance and economics.[5] For those living at the lowest end of the pay scale and who are subject to exorbitant fees by loan sharks, there are distinct dangers in not understanding how compound interest works. It's a problem if a person doesn't know how 30 percent interest tacked on to a debt can make that obligation balloon in no time. If knowledge is power, then the opposite is also true. Ignorance is weakness.

What the poor and underserved don't know presents an opening for others to take advantage of them.

So pulling out cash from an EBT card at a bank ATM is expensive. But it's also bad for the working poor who cash their paychecks and dish out the typical 3 percent fee.[6] Let's ponder the situation faced by the 15 percent of Americans living at the poverty level and making $11,720 a year.[7] Assuming they don't pay taxes up front, they receive a $450 paycheck every other week. If they cash that check at the going rate, they end up paying $13.52 each time. That doesn't sound too bad, until you realize they spent $352 in a single year. Nearly two weeks of work went to just getting their money.

The problem isn't always lack of bank access. Sometimes it's that access to a financial institution also comes with strings attached. In Oregon, if you receive unemployment benefits and don't already have a bank account, your weekly pay is placed on a prepaid U.S. Bank debit card. But as the *Huffington Post* showed in 2011, this is another case in which some welfare money is wasted and doesn't actually go to those who need it.[8] The bank allowed for four free ATM withdrawals per month, but $1.50 fees kicked in after that. For those with little money in the bank and barely any incoming cash flow, frequent trips to the ATM are a must. The fees become practically unavoidable.

It's also becoming popular for low-wage employers to pay their workers with prepaid debit cards. Restaurants and retailers are attracted to it, because they're promised lower costs if they swap paychecks for payroll cards. The downside? Banks charge an array of fees: maybe 50¢ for a card purchase here, another $2 for out-of-network ATM withdrawals there—and one even charges a $7.50 inactivity fee if the account isn't used for 60 days.[9]

In all of these situations, the common theme is that people are paying outsized fees to access their own money. This is exactly the kind of problem addressed by a digital currency that runs on a peer-to-peer network, the way Bitcoin does. Transaction fees are vastly reduced by cutting out middlemen like banks and check cashing stores.

But what good is electronic, Internet money to the poor? As it turns out, many of them already have the means. There's a greater likelihood someone with a lower income will own a cell phone than use a bank account. While 84 percent of those making less than $30,000 a year own a cell phone, only 57 percent use their bank account regularly.[10] It makes sense. Mobile phones have become relatively cheap, even as they've grown in importance as an everyday utility—and replaced landlines. Meanwhile, most of those with lower income use their cell phones to access the Internet. In fact, for many of them it's the primary way to go online, because it's too expensive to keep a computer at home.[11]

The problem with lack of banking access doesn't hit all Americans equally. It hits blacks and Hispanics the worst. The FDIC survey shows that 55 percent of blacks either don't have a bank account or barely use one. Meanwhile, 49 percent of Hispanics endure the same. That stark number—and the hellish financial situation they experience as a result—is the reason two New Yorkers launched a mobile banking platform for Spanish speakers called Refundo. It's mobile banking for those who have had trouble opening accounts on their own. It was an idea that Roger Chinchilla and Grimaldy Dominguez came up with in 2009, when they were running their accounting software startup, Rushtax. They noticed that whenever they asked their customers for a bank account to know where to deposit an IRS tax return, customers would merely shrug.

They had no such thing. The realization hit the guys like a ton of bricks: Latin American families were still going through the same hardships that Chincilla and Dominguez witnessed more than a decade ago growing up together in Queens. As kids, they watched helplessly as Hispanic workers ended every week with a trip to their only financial outlet: check cashing stores. Every visit took a bite out of the paycheck. When it became clear that the Hispanic community remains under-served by banks, Chinchilla and Dominguez decided to take action themselves.

The point of highlighting these circumstances isn't to demonize banks. They still play an important role as the chief source of credit when people want to buy homes, cars and other high-ticket items they can't afford to pay up front. And the switch from actual food stamps and government checks to EBT has actually been quite a success: For users, it's safer than carrying cash or checks. For taxpayers, it's an effective way to track money and ensure the poor aren't spending charitable benefits improperly. The takeaway here is that transaction fees should be less expensive. Presently, they put a damper on the flow of money to people who need it.

But it won't take a brand new, cheaper form of money to push banks out of the welfare and payroll card business. Government and public pressure is already exacting its toll. After folks in New York complained about high bank fees on prepaid payroll cards, State Attorney General Eric Schneiderman fired off letters to 20 banks demanding answers about their programs in 2013. Sometime later, JPMorgan Chase landed a target on its back after it mistakenly mailed 4,000 bad replacement cards to people in Connecticut—and also became the target of hackers who possibly accessed personal data on nearly half a million prepaid card holders. By early 2014, anonymous insiders told

Reuters the bank had plans to leave the prepaid card business. It had become too much of a hassle.[12]

If the poor and working class are forced to return to the old way—cashing paychecks for stiff fees—they aren't any better off. This is where a robust electronic, peer-to-peer money system could make a difference. At a U.S. Senate hearing on Bitcoin in 2013, Massachusetts bank commissioner David Cotney made that very point. Even though he listed the many dangers of having an independent computerized currency—consumer protection, national security, money laundering—he still sees the bright side.

"The potential benefits are similarly multifaceted: speed and efficiency, lower transaction costs, and providing an outlet for the unbanked and underbanked around the world," Cotney told senators.

Indeed, as if these stories aren't difficult enough, remember that the United States is presently the financial capital of the world. It's worse elsewhere. Gallup's global financial inclusion study is telling. Leaving out a few relatively rich nations, the Middle East and North Africa have it worst. Only 18 percent actually have an account at a formal financial institution.[13] Next in line is Sub-Saharan Africa, with 24 percent. In these regions, this problem is well-documented. There's seldom a bank nearby, and pulling out cash leaves a person vulnerable during the long stretch home on highways that—depending on the country—could be rife with bandits or paramilitary groups. In Sudan, there's the more-than-decade-long genocide and war that has claimed 300,000 lives and displaced more than 2.5 million people.[14] In Uganda and the Central African Republic, warlord Joseph Kony continues to wreak havoc with his Lord's Resistance Army of child soldiers (U.S. Special Forces operatives in early 2014 joined the hunt to track him down).[15] These are not environments that are well suited to installing a fleet of ATMs—or walking home with a wad of cash in your pocket.

Indeed, one need not rely on the most drastic tragedies to make the point that Africa is ill-equipped to fully bank its 1 billion people. Look instead to its lack of infrastructure. In Sub-Saharan Africa, only 29 percent of the roads are paved and only one in four people have access to electricity. That immediately increases the difficulty of installing ATMs and making that walk home. Yet 60 percent of those in this region have cell phone coverage.[16] That curious development is what makes Africa a prime spot for the development of electronic money. In fact, it's already well underway.

Kenya's biggest mobile network operator, Safaricom, took a major innovative leap forward in 2007 when it created a low-cost, phone-based payment system, M-PESA. The program works like this: You deposit cash into your mobile account, and that money becomes "e-float" units measured the same way as the currency. Now you can send others that money via SMS. There's no longer a need for trips to the bank every time you want to use your money, and it reduces the likelihood of getting mugged. As New Yorkers pay for their morning coffee by rummaging through their checkbook wallets and fumbling with credit cards and cash, tech-empowered Kenyans doing afternoon shopping simply whip out their cell phones and have store clerks do the same. Send the SMS, and presto! The payment is made.

The program, which exploded in popularity right off the bat, has been a smashing success across Kenya, because it has effectively banked some of the bankless. That is, despite the fact that the country's central bank has had reservations about classifying M-PESA as an actual banking service. By early 2014, Safaricom found that 18 million of its 20 million mobile phone customers use M-PESA.[17] That means the number of folks banking through their cell phones has far surpassed the 8 million or so who own a formal bank account. A surprising statistic: Phone-based money transactions have become such a fundamental part of Kenya's economy that 43 percent of GDP flows through M-PESA.

What's truly impressive is that this caught on despite major structural difficulties. Sure, it's great that 95 percent of Kenya's 41 million people get mobile coverage.[18] But only a quarter of the country lives in areas with a dependable and distributed source of power. The result? There are 19 million mobile subscribers who get phone reception but live off the grid. Think about that odd scenario. That means many people are getting a phone, then have nowhere to charge it. There's even a booming business in setting up charging stations, kind of like when U.S. Internet cafés were all the rage in 1999. But mobile subscribers still manage to make it work, because cell phones and M-PESA have become a fundamental part of everyday living.

These types of digital payments don't only change how people access their hard-earned money. They also affect how people spend it. The main reason is M-PESA's small transaction costs. Safaricom charges a nominal fee for making withdrawals, typically well below the rate charged by Western Union for money transfers. Instead of making fewer deals that are expensive, people tend to make many tiny ones. Examine the difference between the use of checks and mobile payments in Kenya during a one-year period starting in 2007. On an average day, the nation counted 39,000 transactions involving checks, each worth 216 million shillings. Meanwhile, there were 107,000 mobile transactions worth a measly 3 million shillings each.[19] This alone provides a clear case for electronic payments: Shrinking transaction costs lessens the annoyance of moving your money. There's less friction, and hence, less waste.

The manner in which M-PESA is being used also shows why digital money with low transfer costs is the way of the future. Having a widespread digital network lowers the difficulty of sending payments great distances to people in remote areas. Safaricom is well aware of this power. The mobile provider's typical commercial tugs on your heartstrings with the "Send Money Home" tagline; images show young professionals sending remittances to faraway parents. What better way to show your love than sending Mom some cash? In short order, the payment system became a must-have app in Kenya. What was primarily a money transfer service has since evolved slightly into a mobile wallet function as well. Part of that is because Safaricom found itself a competitor: Mobile operator Zain launched Zap money (a service which later became Airtel Money).[20] M-PESA has since expanded to neighboring Tanzania, where the Uchumi supermarket chain now lets customers pay via cell phone.

M-PESA's spectacular results were cited by a representative of the U.S. bank lobby during the Senate Banking Committee's 2013 hearing on Bitcoin. Paul Smocer, who leads the Financial Services Roundtable's technology policy division, told senators that Bitcoin's future success would be measured by its acceptability. And if things went well, digital currencies could follow in M-PESA's path, giving a key service to the underbanked.

It's worth a reminder that M-PESA is not a peer-to-peer currency the way Bitcoin is. The popularity of M-PESA does not imply an independent, nationless money system will meet similar success. But it does show the potential benefits of banking the unbanked—and doing so in a way that's less wasteful than sticking to brick-and-mortar institutions. Kenyans have told researchers they feel safer without having to carry physical cash; there's peace of mind that money sent to family members will actually get there (the old way was stuffing cash in envelopes and sending them via cross-country minibus); and shopkeepers say the conversion to digital cash has made for a more robust marketplace.[21]

Latin America and the Caribbean are also poised to leverage a digital currency revolution, and for the same reason as Africa. The build-out of mobile phone infrastructure has outpaced other services. As of 2012, more than half of the region's 600 million people were subscribed to a cell phone service, and the rate of growth is speeding up.[22] They outnumber the 39 percent who have a formal bank account.[23] So, while most people remain unbanked, they need not be. In fact, twice as many Latin Americans are willing to use their cell phones to make payments than those in the United States or Europe.[24] Brazil provides a great example, where mobile banking caught on in 2010, and more than 3 million people created new user accounts in a single year. The rise of Internet-capable smartphones will be a game-changer, especially because they already make up one in five phones in the region. That's expected to more than double by 2017.

That will make it easier for folks to receive money from abroad, and that's pivotal for a region that so heavily depends on remittances. In fact, the money that Latin American workers in the United States send to poor family members back home is a substantial source of what flows through the financial veins of Latin America. In some countries, it makes up more than 10 percent of GDP.[25] And if you look at the region as a whole, on any given year, migrants send home 250 million money transfers that average about $300 each. The aggregate total actually outweighs all other foreign aid from governments, banks, and charity organizations.

Consider the experience of many immigrants who make their way to the United States and Canada. It's custom for someone who makes the trek, once he or she secures a steady job, to send financial help to parents or siblings struggling back home. A single U.S. dollar goes a long way in a place like Guatemala or Nicaragua. That's what makes it worthwhile to pack up, leave everything and everyone you know, and venture north— even if this new home ends up being unwelcoming and downright exploitative of your labor. This is a point that gets lost on those clamoring for taller fences, heavily armed troops at the U.S.-Mexico border, and crackdowns on illegal immigration. If you pause for a second and think about this through a compassionate lens, it's all about seeking economic opportunity to better the lives of those back home—and make the region more self-sustaining in general.

But there are significant fees for sending money back home via wire services and transfers between banks. The impact gets magnified when every dollar counts. My own family has seen this firsthand. For years, my mother in Florida sent what little money she could to her retired mother in Chile. It averaged about $50 a month. That might not sound like much, but during the winter months it made a huge difference to an elderly woman who could now afford a higher gas utility bill. That meant she could keep the heater on constantly, instead of turning it on only at night and being left to shiver in the cold during the day. For my mother, there was no use trying to send money between bank accounts, because the fees alone—$70 a pop—outweighed the help. Instead, she settled for wiring money via Western Union. That service used a sliding scale of fees, and sending $50 cost her $5. But what if sending money home was cheaper? What if sending $10 at any given time were a frictionless action—and cheaper too? Until I started writing this book, I never thought to ask my mother what a difference it would make if the cost of every transfer were reduced. She said that, in retrospect, she would have broken up her remittance into smaller, weekly payments. It would have given my grandmother a smoother cash flow instead of forcing her to wait for that single deposit every month.

Banking the unbanked—and easing the delivery of money to those who need it most—are the two strongest cases for a digital currency. And I'll be the first to say that it doesn't even need to be Bitcoin. But there's clearly a place for more efficient money that catches up with the pervasive communication networks that already connect us all so well. This potential hasn't been lost on the dinosaurs in the financial industry.

Just as talk about Bitcoin was getting hot in 2013, JPMorgan dusted off a patent for an electronic payment system it had filed more than a decade earlier, added some Bitcoin-like features, and resubmitted it with the U.S. government.[26] At the time, the bank didn't explain the impetus for the move. But a close look at the old patent and this newer application shows that the bank was planting a stake in the ground. JPMorgan acknowledged that there's no efficient way to send money online to people or merchants. Its answer: a system made up of digital wallets, seamless transfers, and anonymity. Sound familiar? There is also a feature that would work as an add-on to Internet browsers, letting you shop online without having to enter credit card information or fill out forms. A so-called "Internet Pay Anyone Account" lets you move money without identifying yourself, and it's as easy as sending an email. Here's how JPMorgan described it: "The credit pushes can be made completely anonymously, with the recipient of the credit having no way to determine from where the credit originated." There's also a feature that online businesses and charities will find useful: a virtual private lockbox. Accepting donations? Publish its address without worrying someone can use that to empty the account. It only accepts funds.

What's most interesting, however, was that the patent application included what sounded like a cross between a stark realization and a confession: The modern financial system is outdated. Transaction fees are just too high. JPMorgan's analysis boiled down to three points. First, debit and credit card fees charged to online merchants, which start at 1.4 percent or higher, are holding them back from selling lots of low-ticket items. It just doesn't make financial sense for the seller, no matter how many shoppers want to buy them. Second, shopping on the Web has evolved, and product makers are now selling directly to customers. They're circumventing retailers, so pricing is more competitive than ever. Every penny counts. In this environment, it doesn't make sense to keep charging so much to facilitate the deal. Third, the digitization of media has made it so consumers are more frequently buying music, movies, and video games online—again, low-cost items that don't make sense with hefty bank surcharges. "A new marketplace has emerged for low-dollar, high-volume, real-time payments," the application said.

It might not be immediately obvious, but opening the floodgates for zillions of tiny transactions will change the world—profoundly.

The Might of Micropayments

Head to the *Financial Times* website (FT.com) and try to peruse through their day's stories. At some point, a message will pop up on your screen that stops you dead in your tracks.

"High quality global journalism requires investment," it says. They're right. Nothing has undercut great reporting quite like the Web—or rather, the terrible business decision news companies made long ago to not charge for their content. Now let's review our options:

Select an access level	Newspaper + Premium online	Premium online Full FT.com subscription	Standard online Full news & archive	Registration 8 articles per month
Price ○ Monthly ● Annual	US$11.50 per week	US$8.99 per week	US$6.25 per week	Free
FT Alphaville plus selected FT blogs	✓	✓	✓	✓
Unlimited FT.com article access	✓	✓	✓	✗
Unlimited mobile and tablet access	✓	✓	✓	✗
Unlimited fastFT	✓	✓	✓	✗
5 year company financials archive	✓	✓	✓	✗
The LEX column	✓	✓	✗	✗
ePaper access	✓	✓	✗	✗
Three exclusive weekly emails	✓	✓	✗	✗
Daily newspaper delivery	✓	✗	✗	✗
FT Weekend delivery	✓	✗	✗	✗

It doesn't seem like too much of a hassle for the most basic online access. And given the excellence of this newspaper's reporting and writing, 89¢ a day is a steal. But unless you're a devoted fan, you're not going to lock yourself into a year-long $325 contract. In fact, this high paywall prevents you from reading *FT*, so you're less likely to become that devoted fan. At least the *New York Times*' website, nytimes.com, allows you 10 free articles a month before a pop-up asks for a $3.75 weekly subscription fee.

It's commendable that some news organizations are finally taking a stand and no longer giving away content for free. Newspapers and magazines have been doing that for more than a decade at their own peril. I've already witnessed several rounds of mass firings at three different newspapers that can attest to the bad results. Seasoned reporters who had a firm grasp of how politics and business works were deemed too expensive to keep on the payroll, especially given their higher wages and benefits.

They were replaced by interns and per diem employees, young and inexperienced, who could churn out short news posts and would not demand health insurance. This cost-slashing happened repeatedly as news organizations struggled to keep up with the drop in advertising revenue—fueled by the fact that readers could get their news for free online. During a particularly rough patch between 2007 and 2012, the United States lost 27 percent of its full-time journalists, bringing the total who still had a job to 38,000 nationwide.[27] Considering the civic role we play in relaying information to the citizenry, that left roughly one lone reporter to cover the laws, actions, and functions of each local government. And that's assuming journalists ignored state and federal government, as well as all business, science, and art.

The water-cooler conversations that went on in every newsroom went something like this:

> **JOURNALIST 1:** Print is dead. The industry is doomed. We're all going to lose our jobs.
>
> **JOURNALIST 2:** What did we expect? We don't charge for anything on our site, and the ad revenue doesn't pay enough.
>
> **JOURNALIST 3:** But we can't raise a paywall. No one's going to buy in. They'll just get their news from news aggregators like Yahoo or AOL. It's a race to the bottom.

What got lost in these conversations, however, is that the way we currently handle money is one of the reasons paywalls are so high—and why some folks won't pay for them. Currently, credit-card processing fees attached to each online purchase form a price floor, a minimum that company needs to charge in order for the deal to be profitable. But if those surcharges take a smaller slice of each purchase, it suddenly becomes feasible to pay as you go—in finite fragments.

To properly consider a working scenario, imagine three elements. The first is a functioning digital currency, like Bitcoin, that can be broken down into infinitesimal parts. The second is an add-on to your Web browser that automatically pays whatever website you visit a pre-designated amount anytime you read an article. For the sake of simplicity, let's say it's equivalent to 10¢. Depending on your reading habits, that might not even give you pause. The third is that news organizations accept those incoming payments. Again for simplicity, price competition means that they all charge about the same: 10¢ per story. Let's add it all up. Throughout your day you read a few news articles; some on your phone, others at your work computer, a few at home. Without giving it a second thought, each time you click, a dime gets deducted from your account. Even when you stop to think about it, you don't mind paying whatever that was, maybe 90¢ a day. Your lunch was more expensive. Hell, the detour you took after work cost you more in gas than that. And besides, it sure seems like a bargain when you consider that it paid all those hard-working journalists who just informed you about the new treatment for diabetes, details about an upcoming debate on taxes, and the latest hot stocks.

Wait a minute. That comes out to $328.50 a year. Isn't that about the cost of the *Financial Times* subscription described above? It sure is. But you didn't pay the *FT* alone. Every news site that contributed something worth reading got its fair share. In fact, so did a few small-time bloggers who wrote something memorable or broke some incredibly important news.

Some call it "micropayments." Others say "nanopayments." Regardless of the scale, it's a hotly debated issue among technologists, because the concept is expected to catch on, and its effects will be revolutionary. Entrepreneurs who independently produce media that gets consumed online—news, fiction stories, poetry, music, photography, graphic art—have a better shot of getting paid for it. By distributing payments more evenly across all media producers, micropayments give your local, dedicated blogger better footing. Her blog post probably won't be seen by as many readers as the average piece on nytimes. com, but at least she'll be compensated for it. That, in effect, democratizes the payment process, so an independent journalist has an equal chance of getting paid for her work. She doesn't have to suffer and give away content for free just because she's independently employed. The same goes for musicians who share their compositions online for others to download. Sure, the Web is rife with media piracy and duplicated mp3s. It's easy to grab an entire album and not pay for it. But wouldn't you pay 10¢ for a song if you knew every penny went to the artist and not the corporations that sit between you both?

It's worth noting that this system doesn't exist right now. Independent journalists and artists can't charge you 10¢ per story, because fees levied by PayPal and banks make it impossible. If you're a blogger making $3,000 per month and use PayPal, the service charges 30¢ for every transaction, plus a 2.9 percent fee.[28] It's not exorbitant by any means, but it doesn't allow for micropayments.

Consumers arguably would be better off, because a micropayment system properly attributes your consumption. You don't overpay. And as different forms of media gravitate toward the Web, the same reasoning applies to all sorts of things. Imagine if you only paid for the television programs you actually wanted to watch. The entire industry would undergo a dramatic shift. Networks would have to rethink how they fund programs. When viewers stop watching a certain show (and therefore paying), networks might be more likely to cancel that program sooner. Then again, programs with a dedicated audience of paying fans are more likely to stick around. It's difficult to say whether quality programming would win out over brainless reality shows, but one thing is for sure: It's a democratic process, and the one with greater support wins.

However, there's at least one obvious downside to micropayments for businesses. By providing smaller funds in a more widely distributed fashion, they also make for increased volatility in revenue. When I paid my $99 annual subscription to the *Economist*, the publication received my money up front and was better able to assess its current finances and plan its business in the coming months. If I paid per story, it would be immensely more difficult to plan ahead. Then again, by vastly lowering the difficulty and annoyance of payment, the news magazine is more likely to receive a steadier flow of revenue.

At least for the news industry, the emergence of digital currency is well timed. For all the cynicism about actually charging customers for reading content, news sites are finally embracing paywalls. By mid-2013, more than 500 of the 1,400 daily publications in the United States had instituted them.[29] Lo and behold, revenue from circulation grew for the second straight year.

The first major newspaper to venture into uncharted territory was the *Chicago Sun-Times*, which erected a Bitcoin paywall in April 2014.[30] A careful look at the company's decision shows that the paper is merely dipping its toes into the water. For instance, the *Sun-Times* partnered with the Bitcoin transaction processer Coinbase, allowing the newspaper to vastly minimize its risk of exposure to volatile bitcoins because it never has to actually hold them. For a nominal fee, Coinbase converts the day's Bitcoin payments into dollars and sends them to the merchant every 24 hours. More relevant to our discussion, though, is that the *Sun-Times* has not offered pay-as-you-go micropayments. The new deal is merely that you can now pay your yearly subscription in Bitcoin. Here's what it looked like on its site. Customers have the choice to either send a payment to the listed address or whip out their cell phones and scan the QR code at the left.

Still, just the fact that a recognizable entity took that step forward shows a willingness to experiment. In a corporate statement, editor-in-chief Jim Kirk said he aims to "keep the *Sun-Times* current and evolving with changing technology. Accepting bitcoin payments is one of many ways we are working to stay digitally focused."

If micropayments do catch on, it will probably develop from online tipping. Some of that already exists, but it's sparse and uncoordinated. Occasionally, hackers (particularly those who claim to do a public service) accept bitcoins as tokens of gratitude. For example, one is a mysterious vigilante who calls himself Jester (JƎSTƎR, to be more accurate). For the sake of brevity, just think Batman for the online world. He's a pro-U.S. military type who takes down Al Qaeda–related websites, attacks servers that host them, and seeks vengeance on whistleblowers who have exposed U.S. government secrets. On his personal site, jesterscourt.cc, he directs would-be supporters to donate to the United States' Wounded Warrior Project or the

United Kingdom's Help for Heroes. But if they insist on sending him money directly, they can ship it to his Bitcoin wallet.

Formalized Bitcoin tipping services have popped up here and there, but none has become substantial. The first popular one, YouTipIt, was launched by a few computer programmers as a side project in 2010. But it shut down two years later when it ran out of money and started coming under scrutiny by Germany's finance regulator.[31] Another, BTCTip, appeared as a "Twitter-based microtipper," but the beta service ran into problems after a website security breach.[32] The latest is Tipper-Coin, an automated service that lets you easily tip someone on Twitter if you like something they said. What hasn't yet flourished as a system, however, is the digital currency equivalent of effortlessly dropping a coin in someone's tip jar—no matter where you go.

When I start thinking about it that way, my mind immediately goes to musicians. Becoming a full-time composer and performer increasingly looks like a nowhere road, especially in the post-Napster age. Theft of artistic work has put financial pressure on record companies, which ultimately means more pressure on musicians themselves. I've talked about this with dozens of professional musicians ranging from local bands in New York clubs to European metal rock stars. And I'll admit that I too have received ripped mp3s from friends. We all have. But even our traditional payment systems aren't enough to undo the damage. The prospect of surviving as an independent musician is still untenable today, even as fans pay for individual songs via iTunes and Amazon or stream free music on Pandora, which pays royalty fees through advertising.

There have already been a few cases in which artists circumvent distributors, like record companies, and go directly to their fans. It worked for Radiohead in 2007, when the British band released the album *In Rainbows* online for free a few months before its physical release, asking fans to "pay what you wish." As expected, piracy went through the roof.[33] More than 2 million copies were swapped online for free on platforms like BitTorrent in the first month of its release. And most fans got off without paying at all. But upon release of its physical disc, the 10-track album immediately topped the Billboard chart and went on to generate more sales than the band's 2003 album *Hail to the Thief*. In the first year, the band sold 3 million copies in CDs, paid downloads, and special edition box sets.[34]

What micropayments can really do, though, is add fuel to the kind of fire that's kindled by performers like Amanda Palmer. The punk-cabaret musician is adamant about directly connecting to her fans and offering her music for free, with the unspoken agreement that if you love it, support it. She famously raised close to $1.2 million directly from fans on the crowdfunding website Kickstarter in 2012. In an impassioned TED talk the next year, she laid out a vision of the future, in which musicians discard with the concept of "celebrity" that keeps fans at a distance and instead connect with them directly, especially for financial contributions.[35] "I think people have been obsessed with the wrong question, which is: How do we make people pay for music?" she said during that TED talk. "What if we started asking: How do we let people pay for music?" Lessening the difficulty to send money their way takes a big step toward making that happen.

Can it really work, though? The best example yet is the touching tale of how the Jamaican bobsled team made it to the 2014 Winter Olympics. The team had no chance of traveling to Sochi in Russia, because unlike their competitors from rich nations who had lucrative corporate sponsorships, they were broke. But the idealistic Internet community came to the rescue. It was driven by nostalgia over the 1993 movie *Cool*

Runnings, the underdog Disney film about how a real-life group of athletes living on an island where the average temperature is 85° Fahrenheit managed to compete in a sport designed specifically for sub-freezing climates. And it worked. In just 12 hours, users of the wacky digital currency Dogecoin raised nearly $25,000—enough to help the team make the trip.[36]

While I've focused on those in creative professions, it won't be long before politicians get wind of this as well. Just think about how often you get passionate about a certain political issue, say, school funding or gun rights. What if, during a politician's election bid, you could send a few cents their way with a simple click? On April 17, 2014, Texas Attorney General Greg Abbott became the first politician to accept bitcoins as contributions to his campaign for state governor. In the days that followed, most reports focused on how this Republican is catering to the free market crowd. But just beneath the surface is the hint that campaign finance could be in for a remarkable change. If it's easier and faster to raise lots of money in tiny donations from many people, politicians have less incentive to rely so heavily on a few, powerful donors—and more reason to raise it from the voters themselves.

Privacy in the Age of Big Data

Another major selling point for Bitcoin is its ability to hide who you are during a transaction. You buy what you want, sellers get their money, and everyone's happy. There's no need to know who each other is. But who cares if your purchases can be done with near anonymity? Isn't that only for people buying illegal stuff?

Anyone who takes that cavalier attitude toward shopping privacy should better acquaint themselves with the kind of data collection that takes place—and the potential there for real damage. If you've gone out shopping anytime in the last few years, you've surely run into the following scenario. You reach the cashier, swipe your credit card, then the cashier asks for your zip code.

As any person would, you ask, "What for?"

"It's for marketing purposes," they say; or perhaps, "It's just for internal use." What you don't hear is that the retail shop has struck a deal with another company that will match the name on your credit card to your zip code. That narrows it down to maybe one person. If it's correct, this retailer now knows where you live. But they actually know much more than that.

Nearly all major retailers have ongoing deals with marketing companies that are experts at finding out everything they can about you, the consumer. That information comes from a relatively new type of company, one that doesn't ever get talked about at the dinner table: data brokers. But you should know them, because they know you. And they're changing the world.

Data brokers do exactly what their name implies: They collect and sell information about you—all kinds of it. Much of it is publicly available, such as your name and address. The rest comes from private companies you've done business with before—such as car dealerships and hunting catalogs—that are willing to sell information about your transaction with them. The consequence is a lively, thriving, and quickly growing market that—unbeknownst to you—buys and sells your name, address, birthday, credit score, employment history, estimated salary, recent purchases, and much more.

All you did was give up your zip code, and now this clothing store knows that you missed a credit card payment last Christmas, and you never did pay that parking ticket in Atlanta. That's a problem, because these retailers are preyed upon by hackers who tap into their databases and steal your personal details. Target experienced that during the 2013 holiday shopping season, when it lost data on up to 110 million Americans. That's a third of the country. The same thing happened to millions who shopped at Michaels craft stores and Neiman Marcus.

There's a term for those unfathomably deep oceans of information that these companies are collecting, buying, selling and analyzing: Big Data. It doesn't necessarily just refer to your personal details. That information could be just about anything: temperature at specific locations around the globe, the volume of car traffic in a given city, viewership numbers for a TV show, etc. It's something I discuss constantly with major corporations, researchers, and experts in academia, because there are two major issues at play. The first is that there is incredible potential to advance science, increase efficiency, avoid calamities, and better tailor our lives to our personal preferences. The other is that it erodes our privacy—and that's where a cryptocurrency like Bitcoin comes in. By anonymizing transactions, Bitcoin allows you to shield yourself from this kind of data collection at the source: your interaction with merchants.

Most of our direct interaction with Big Data consists of low-hanging fruit, the easy stuff. Retailers want to track our purchases, because it helps them more efficiently stock store shelves and better direct their advertising. There's clearly value in that, because companies are willing to pay you for it. That explains the discount you get with that membership card to that national pharmacy chain. It's tracking all your purchases. The occasional rebate is your compensation.

So what's the downside? For starters, the swapping of our most personal details happens behind closed doors, so we don't know how it's shared or who acquires it. No one I've ever met actually reads every contract they encounter when they sign up for email, social media, smartphone apps, and streaming media services. If you've never combed through one, this might be a surprise. The vast majority of these end-user license agreements (Silicon Valley simply refers to them as EULAs) give a company permission to share the data they gather about you with others. And you can be absolutely sure they do. But there are currently no disclosure laws that force anyone to let you know how you're being torn apart, sown back together, bought, and sold.

I had breakfast with Gary Kovacs, who led Mozilla as CEO as it developed the Firefox Web browser, to talk about this issue. He's passionate about privacy (Mozilla was named "Most Trusted Internet Company" of 2012) and is concerned about third parties that track your online activity. That became especially true after he found out that several companies were tracking his own daughter while she surfed online—on kids' websites, nonetheless. Here's how he described the industry for your data:

"It's a black market," he said. "No one knows exactly what's going on."

But we do occasionally get a glimpse. It's not pretty.

Just after New Year's Day in 2014, a couple living in the Chicago suburbs got a nondescript letter from OfficeMax.[37] It looked like the usual junk mail. Except this time, it was addressed this way:

Mike Seay

Daughter Killed in Car Crash

Or Current Business

The couple was shocked. It had been less than a year since they lost their 17-year-old daughter. Ashley was with her boyfriend when their SUV slid off the road, crashed into a tree and killed them both. Somehow, this company knew. But more importantly, this mail showed that somewhere out there, some unnamed company had built a personal file on the Seay family—documented its tragedy—and thought it relevant enough to keep in its marketing profiles. Seay called the company demanding an apology. OfficeMax said it was sorry and later admitted that it had teamed up with a third-party firm for its mailing.

"Why would they have that kind of information? Why would they need that?" Seay told a local television reporter. "And how much more information, if they have that, do they have on me or anyone else?"

That's one example that shows how the consumer data collected is sometimes misused. But there's something bigger to worry about. If your aggregated data gets into the wrong hands, it becomes absolutely dangerous. And I'm not talking about some genius hacker breaking into a company's server. That sad truth is that if they pose as a legitimate company, they can just buy it.

As of this writing, the U.S. Secret Service and the top prosecutors of Florida, Illinois, and several other states are investigating how a Vietnamese hacker managed to obtain sensitive consumer data from one of the three big credit bureaus, Experian. According to court documents and my interviews with those familiar with the case, a young man living in Vietnam named Hieu Minh Ngo masqueraded as a genuine company and struck a deal with one of the many relatively unknown data aggregators of U.S. public records, Court Ventures. Armed with that batch of information, Ngo launched an identity theft website where others could buy the names, Social Security numbers and much more on millions of Americans. In 2012 Experian acquired Court Ventures. It wasn't until Secret Service agents started investigating mysterious wire transfers coming from Southeast Asia that any of this became apparent. Ngo was arrested in Guam and pled guilty to three fraud-related counts in March 2014.[38]

And now for your second glimpse into the world of data brokers. When news of this broke in April 2014, another data aggregator, U.S. Info Search, was dragged into the spotlight because it was feeding data to Court Ventures, which fed data to Experian, which fed data to Ngo.

This hints at how interconnected and complex the swapping of your personal information really is. And even if one data broker is responsible, all it takes is one weak link in the chain to put you at risk. It turns out that Ngo had long ago tried to buy data from this small, Columbus, Ohio–based firm but was turned away. However, because U.S. Info Search had an ongoing agreement to provide data to Court Ventures, Ngo got what he wanted anyway.

Angered by the fact that Experian kept directing media attention to U.S. Info Search, the small firm CEO Marc Martin posted a lengthy note on April 7 blasting the credit giant.[39] "Experian sold data to an identity thief, and now expects someone else to pay for notifications and credit monitoring," he said. Martin also accused Experian of not properly notifying victims that their data was exposed, and hiding the extent of the damage. But one thing in his letter stands out above all the rest: his description of Experian's services (edited for grammatical errors). Keep in mind, this is a former client he's talking about—one that his firm fed with your information:

> Experian not only sells credit reports, but makes a good profit from routinely selling their entire credit file of U.S. residents to companies around the world via "licensing agreements." And many of these companies in turn sell the data to other people and companies. This data can include SSNs, driver's license info, DOBs, employment, relatives, and much more.

Martin declined to speak with me to elaborate on what I've already described, as did Experian. But the court documents make the point clearly enough. There's a lot of data flowing around in dark places we can't see, sold to folks we don't know, who do with it whatever they please.

A digital currency like Bitcoin has the potential to replace credit cards—which have your name etched into the magnetic stripe for all to see—with a payment system that can keep its users from knowing one another. The seller doesn't have to know who you are. If they don't know anything about you, they have nothing to collect, amass, exploit, and put at risk. It won't stop the collection of all your publicly recorded details, but at least you can keep your purchases to yourself.

A Record for When It Matters

Bitcoin might be nameless, but it's not entirely anonymous. Buyers and sellers never have to share identifying information about one another except for their digital wallet addresses. However, the system's public accounting book, the block chain, records every transaction for all to see. It might seem counterintuitive—a system of money that's totally traceable offers heightened privacy. But it all comes down to who knows which digital wallet is yours. That gives law enforcement an effective tool for hunting down criminals, should they ever connect the dots between a digital wallet and its real-life owner.

That's why it's utterly stupid to conduct illegal activities with bitcoins. It's a wonder why so many people who buy drugs or other illicit goods online think they'll get away with it in the long run. To anyone even remotely familiar with the way Bitcoin works, this is old news. But its pervasive use in the online black market (which I'll expand on later) is sufficient evidence that few have yet to fully grasp the concept. If people understood its potential for law enforcement, there'd be less talk about how Bitcoin is great for laundering money and more talk about how anyone conducting illegal activities with bitcoins is a fool. All it takes is having the right rules put in place and thorough forensics following Bitcoin-related drug busts. In that sense, bitcoins are the equivalent of irradiated bills like the ones used by investigators taking down major crime syndicates. The proof of guilt is the money in your possession.

The way to do that, according to several financial regulators, is to start tracking digital wallets when people receive their first bitcoin. In other words: at the exchanges. That's where most newcomers enter the world of virtual money, so it makes for a good security checkpoint. By applying the same know-your-customer rules already in place at banks, law enforcement connects a name to a wallet. From there on, an irrevocable map is drawn that follows your every financial move. But that information doesn't need to be shared with everyone else, much in the same way that a person's financial investments are personal information and don't need to be broadcasted to the world.

This is what smart governments—the ones that are proactively setting up rules to accommodate digital currencies—are grappling with right now. The subject of anonymity came up multiple times during the Senate Banking Committee hearing in late 2013. The meeting was meant as a way to get politicians up to speed on digital currencies, so Bitcoin was lumped in with E-Gold and Liberty Reserve, two experiments in electronic money that ended when they were shut down by law enforcement for being large money laundering operations. In some ways, that association was useful because the same dangers persist. Criminals online are indeed flocking to Bitcoin, because it's hard to trace without the enforcement of the most basic know-your-customer regulation. But the reason that isn't around is because governments haven't yet held digital currencies to a higher standard and treated them as real-life money. If they did, users would be subject to the same scrutiny as credit cards, allowing police to look back and comb through all of your spending.

At the hearing, a U.S. Secret Service representative, Special Agent Edward Lowery III, told senators that international criminal organizations are drawn to digital currencies because they operate largely in the shadows and are, by their very nature, transnational. That highlights the need for governments to act in unison on this issue. Ernie Allen, president of the International Centre for Missing and Exploited Children, explained that distributors of child pornography use bitcoins and other digital currencies, because of "a perception of anonymity." But as Allen astutely noted, "If the perception of anonymity diminishes, we believe the criminal use will diminish with it."

The way to do away with that perception is to make two points clear to consumers: Bitcoin makes you anonymous when you're shopping, but not to the law. That's why Mythili Raman, one of the federal government's top prosecutors, told senators, "To be clear, virtual currency is not necessarily synonymous with anonymity. A convertible virtual currency with appropriate anti–money laundering and know-your-customer controls, as required by U.S. law, can safeguard its system from exploitation by criminals and terrorists in the same way any other money services business could."

There's already a bright scholar that's looking into the matter, and she's poised to be the go-to expert for the FBI, INTERPOL, and others in the years to come. Sarah Meiklejohn started researching the ability to trace bitcoins while earning her PhD in computer science at the University of California in

San Diego. Her interest in security and cryptography led her to wonder whether Bitcoin's public ledger could be used to identify spending patterns. She teamed up with colleagues at UCSD and George Mason University, got a few grants from the National Science Foundation and the Office of Naval Research, and set off to look into the matter.

Meiklejohn discovered that by monitoring the block chain and making occasional Bitcoin purchases herself, she could cluster thousands of digital wallets together and figure out who were the operators. On the drug-selling website Silk Road, for instance, Meiklejohn made fewer than a dozen transactions and was able to spot 295,435 digital wallets that used that service.[40] Her research team could also identify individual markets, knowing the difference between exchanges Mt.Gox and BTC-e.

The team's conclusion sounds like a warning to would-be criminals: "An agency with subpoena power would be well placed to identify who is paying money to whom."[41]

For all the talk about Bitcoin being a bastion for bandits, it's more like a boon for anyone wearing a badge. Imagine the situation that follows if someone gets caught receiving mail order drugs from a Bitcoin deal. Police can check out that person's digital wallet, figure out who received money to ship the drugs and have immediate proof they can show in court. Criminals are better off lurking on the streets with cash in their pockets, Meiklejohn told me. Bitcoin has a long—and perfect—memory of everything you've ever done.

"When you go buy drugs with cash, you get caught in one transaction. That's all they can prosecute you on," Meiklejohn said. "If you get caught buying drugs on Silk Road and they look at your transaction history, you get caught on every transaction you've made. It's much more serious."

If only law enforcement is given permission to connect your name to your digital wallet, this would allow for better privacy in the marketplace and more effective criminal investigations.

There are currently limits to forensics, though. Online black markets that sit as middlemen to illegal transactions have employed a "Bitcoin tumbler" that moves money around so it's harder to track bitcoins from buyer to seller. Without a mandate that identifies individual wallet holders, the Meiklejohn method of clustering can only track down what marketplace took your bitcoins—not necessarily who eventually received them as payment. But the potential that already exists isn't lost on law enforcement agencies. Some have already reached out to Meiklejohn for advice. And financial regulators are currently devising rules that will force exchanges to keep records of their customers.

"Every bitcoin is by nature a marked bill. All that's required is putting together some pieces—like getting the exchanges involved," Meiklejohn said.

Money with Strings Attached

If there's one aspect of digital currency that gets overlooked with consistency, it's the unique feature that the money is programmable. That quality makes it distinct from the physical money we know today. Paper dollar bills and gold are physical objects that have value all on their own, and they retain that value no matter where they are or how they're used (in everyday peaceful life, anyway). Physical money bestows power and wealth on others merely by being in their possession. You wouldn't doubt someone sitting on a mound of gold coins is rich. The treasure heap is hers, and she can spend it as she pleases. But computerized money is different, because it's really just software that abides by a certain set of rules, a protocol. Those rules can be adjusted at a moment's notice. All it takes is rewriting the code. It's sort of like inscribing rules onto a gold bar or a paper bill. This essentially turns money into a contract.

There's already something in real life that vaguely resembles this: bearer bonds. Although most folks have never touched one, a bearer bond is a kind of document that promises to pay a predetermined amount to whoever holds it. Technically speaking, it's a debt security typically issued by a business or government. They all say something to the effect of, "This bearer bond promises to pay the bearer X dollars upon settlement of this bond." In the world of contracts, it's great for anonymity, because anyone can cash it out. But for the sake of comparison with virtual currency, it doesn't hold up. Bearer bonds aren't money, and the rules only apply at one entity, like a specific bank.

Digital currency can take rules a step further, because it's entirely customizable. Whoever creates it—or issues it to someone else—can tell it to perform a certain way. No matter what instructions are written onto a paper dollar bill or a gold bar, you can ignore it. But a virtual unit of money could be restricted to only work on weekends. Or at certain shops. Or in a particular person's possession. The possibilities are endless.

It's this aspect of virtual money that most excites Dan Kaufman, the director of information innovation at the Defense Advanced Research Projects Agency. That's quite something, considering this is the man responsible for identifying the most amazing, cutting-edge technology projects at the U.S. military's top research lab. Why would someone who works with the Defense Department be interested in something like Bitcoin? Because money is power, but control over how that money is spent is better than that. It's authority—and that means it can root out bad behavior.

Over dinner with a few reporters in New York, Kaufman explained how very rudimentary versions of this already exist: restricted prepaid debit cards. His son attends college at the University of Maryland, where something called the Terrapin Express program allows students using a special card to buy food, books, and other things on campus. But "Terp dollars" can't buy alcohol. So Kaufman can periodically fill up his son's card without having to worry about subsidizing rounds of beer pong.

"I know he's going to do bad shit, but I feel like he should earn that himself," he joked. "Terp dollars are awesome. I put some money in his account. It can only buy good things. So, I started thinking about foreign aid."

In its current state, foreign aid doesn't work, Kaufman said. It's difficult to ensure that money appropriated for disaster relief isn't diverted elsewhere, and even then, there's little recourse. The money has been spent. There's a lot of history to back this up. One recent example is Afghanistan, which receives more than $1 billion in U.S. aid each year. Corruption and waste are so prevalent that the U.S. government hired independent auditors to look it over in 2011. Their conclusion, made public in early 2014, was that the government can't trust a single one of Afghanistan's 16 ministries.[42] The United States has run into the same problem with Pakistan, where it gave more than $200 million after 2001 on the condition it would be used to fight terror. By 2009, most of it had been used instead on large-scale weaponry like antimissile defense systems and naval-targeting armaments that do nothing to fight off rifle-wielding insurgents but a lot to fuel the military buildup against neighboring India.[43] But at least governments can apply political pressure as retaliation. All the vaccination charity Gavi could do in 2012 when it discovered Sierra Leone officials were overpaying for ambulances and buying themselves lavish cars was simply cut off aid.[44]

The problem is exacerbated, because of the current limitations of money. Kaufman used this example: The United States sends money to a dictator, stipulating that the funds are meant for buying his starving people wheat. Instead, he sends it to his personal Swiss bank account.

"What can I do?" Kaufman said. "Well, I can yell at him. I can sanction him. I can write letters to him. I can threaten him. But it's all kind of bullshit, right? And then I can go over to the Swiss, and they're like, 'Money is money, my friend. It's not our war.'"

All the journalists in the room burst out laughing.

"You can't enforce morality," Kaufman said, shaking his head. "You just can't."

He then clasped his hands together and raised an eyebrow. "Now imagine the following. I invent a new currency, and I can do foreign aid in this currency. And you buy wheat, or you buy a school bus, or you buy purified water, or whatever. Build a mosque—whatever cool thing you want to do."

Except this new money is digital, and it does what you tell it to do. It only works if it's spent as permitted. So when that dictator wires it to his Swiss bank account, it never goes in that direction. It just sits there in his original bank account, waiting to get spent the right way. Now the United States doesn't have to chase after anyone. The money does the job of enforcement all on its own.

"The protocol is everything," I said.

"That's right," Kaufman responded. "I've found the right protocol, and I've done the right encryption on it, so now I don't have to ask the Swiss to do anything they don't want to do... magic money, right?"

No one at DARPA is actively working on something like this yet, Kaufman said. But there's certainly an appetite for this.

A Runaway Inflation Escape Pod

If there's one reason above all others why Bitcoin is a Libertarian dream, it's because the currency is independent of state control. No government determines how many bitcoins are produced. The system regulates itself. It's a simple concept, but it's attempting the biggest power grab in modern financial history. Rogue money is as antiauthority as it gets.

Governments everywhere jealously guard their currencies, because it gives them economic control. The license to create and destroy money is powerful. It affects prices and interest rates, which collectively determine how you get paid, buy things, save money, and invest. That covers just about everything in the economy.

The ones in charge of this task are central bankers. To them, the nation's economy is akin to a machine. To keep it working properly, buttons must be pushed. Levers must be pulled. The most important gauge is the supply of money. That's the fuel. If the economy gets too slow, they hit the gas pedal and pump more petrol into the engine. If it's going too fast, they cut off the fuel and hit the brakes. This control gives central bankers the ability to steer the economy—and avert financial disaster.

When they flood the system with cash, we can thank them for the economic policies that create easy money and lower interest rates: abruptly making our salaries higher and home loans affordable. We can also curse them when those same policies make cheeseburgers more expensive and our savings accounts lose their value. That rise in prices is inflation, the manmade economic condition that comes from the devaluing of your dollar. You could say it's like a hangover. We're addicted to the immediate high of easy money, and we pay for it later with a case of delirium tremens.

This authority has almost always belonged exclusively to governments, but there have been brief periods in which independent institutions have had their own money. Just over a century ago, it was common for a bank to create its own notes that represented value stored in a vault somewhere. This started to change in the late 1800s, when national governments around the globe awarded specific banks a special privilege: the right to issue notes for the entire country.[45] Since then, central bankers have led us into booms and busts that—depending on whom you ask—make them heroes or villains.

There are those who question whether central banks should even have this power. Their voices grew even louder after the Great Recession of 2007–2009, because governments were seen as complicit in fueling the housing bubble. As the United States gripped with the aftermath of a period of easy money, the policies were criticized by two distinct groups on opposite ends of the political spectrum: the Tea Party on the far right and the Occupy movement on the far left. While they disagreed vehemently on immigration policy and state funding of welfare programs, they both came to the conclusion that the federal government had abused its monopoly on the supply of money. Libertarians like the two-time Republican presidential candidate Ron Paul, now a retired congressman, have called to end the Federal Reserve.

Such a drastic change won't come easily—if it ever comes at all. The prevailing view by modern economists is that central bankers serve a useful role manning the machine. Neither political party, Democrat or Republican, has any intention to dissolve the nation's central bank. No other major country is considering that either. But Bitcoin presents a workaround: a competing currency. Instead of yanking the levers away from central bankers, Bitcoin creates something outside their control.

To be clear, the point of an independent digital money is not about avoiding taxes. It is about having a currency people can run to when they're fleeing inflation. It's a lifeboat on a sinking cruise.

Do we really need an escape pod? Is it really that bad? In most places, the answer is no. Most of us are unfamiliar with inflation that spirals out of control. Modern, developed countries have not seen hyperinflation in decades, and there's a general sentiment among central bankers right now that they've learned to tame that beast. But one need not look back too far to see that this monster remains with us.

Zimbabwe's recent monetary crisis sounds like something out of a first-year college economics course. When Zimbabwe shed its colonial name of Rhodesia in 1980 and became an independent state, its new Zimbabwean dollar was more valuable than the U.S. dollar. It had a small, nascent economy, so its largest currency denomination was the Z$20.[46] But government spending went unchecked. It approved bonuses for 60,000 independence war veterans in 1997 without ever budgeting for it. President Robert Mugabe found himself in the awkward situation of digging into empty coffers. He tried raising taxes, but that didn't work, because trade unions protested. The government resorted instead to the less prudent option: Simply print the money. That's how the veterans got paid. And it's how, the very next year, it also funded its participation in the Democratic Republic of the Congo's civil war. Over the next decade, inflation mounted. The government began printing ever higher denominations of currency. Prices skyrocketed. What could buy you a dozen cars in 1998 only paid for a loaf of bread in 2008.[47] A billion Zim dollars got you a bag of coffee. Businesses were forced to raise their employees' wages too, but they always lagged behind, so everyone felt poorer anyway.

The unforgettable moment came in 2009, when the government issued the 100 trillion dollar bill. The eyes just glaze over the zeros: $100,000,000,000,000. That's 14 of them you just skimmed. The currency was clearly worthless. Zimbabwe had become a nation of starving billionaires. Within weeks, Zimbabweans ditched their paper and operated solely on U.S. dollars and South African rands.

This kind of outrageous situation isn't limited to upstarts under dictatorial control in the poorest corner of the globe. How about Argentina? With coveted attributes like ample coastline, cattle and copper, the South American nation is a commercial powerhouse. The sum value of its economic output ranks it near Sweden and Norway. A century ago, it was poised to lead the world's economy. But the country has experienced what the *Economist* has slyly dubbed "one hundred years of ineptitude."[48] The worst of the decline came in the form of rampant hyperinflation which started in the 1970s and peaked in 1989 at 4,923 percent a year.[49] At its darkest hour, food prices rose so quickly that people resorted to riots and looted stores.

To hear about what this was like, I reached out to Mario Diament, one of my college journalism professors at Florida International University. He experienced the financial turmoil firsthand during the 1980s, when he wrote political analysis pieces for a weekly magazine in Buenos Aires. The value of his country's peso was in free-fall.

"The rate of the Argentine peso to the U.S. dollar was changing by the hour," he said. "Everyone knew prices were changing. Children knew."

At supermarkets, the price labels on products were marked over and raised several times a day. Car dealerships, knowing that today's pesos would soon be worthless, promised to pay you back in three months every cent you paid today. But in 90 days, whatever you spent on your car "was now the value of an hour's worth of parking," Diament recalled. When workers received their monthly salary check, they would race to the nearest currency exchange to swap it for U.S. dollars, which retained their value by comparison. Stores still took pesos, so a curious daily ritual appeared. Shoppers would head to an exchange just before the day's activities, and swap their U.S. dollars for only as many pesos as needed. The smartest shoppers returned to the exchange two or three times a day to minimize the loss in their money's value. Hearing this, I was taken aback by the waste of time, effort, and fuel. This is madness. "Yes it is," Diament replied.

This is why some people find the mere thought of inflation so repulsive. Margaret Thatcher, Great Britain's former prime minister, described inflation as "an insidious moral evil" in her 1980 speech before that country's Conservative and Unionist Party.

"Inflation destroys nations and societies as surely as invading armies do," she said. "Inflation is the parent of unemployment. It is the unseen robber of those who have saved. No policy which puts at risk the defeat of inflation—however great its short-term attraction—can be right."

This is where Bitcoin comes in. Its protocol says that only so many bitcoins are produced each year. The system is never at risk of a sudden flood of brand new money. By its very design, Bitcoin is anti-inflationary. So, just like Argentines fled to the U.S. dollar, anyone afraid that their currency is losing value can flock to Bitcoin. It's a refuge currency.

"That's the holy grail for people who believe in freer markets and currency," Adam Gurri told me. He's a Libertarian economics writer for the *Umlaut*, an online journal that discusses innovation and public policy.

Like so many of Bitcoin's other aspects, there's nothing quite like this right now. The closest thing to it worldwide is gold. Have you ever dozed off on the couch watching TV, only to wake up at 3:00 AM in a sleepy stupor? If so, then you've probably caught those cash-for-gold, hour-long infomercials. You know the ones: An older, distinguished-looking man walking through a Palm Beach retirement community tries to sell you the idea that the economy is headed for the tank and your savings are only safe if they're kept in 438.9-ounce gold bars. The problem is, you have to go through a broker. And they take a cut. And it's awfully difficult to break up gold bars to make payments. And no one takes gold as payment anyway.

What's truly revolutionary, though, is what happens if a large portion of the population ditches their dollars for bitcoins. If enough people become currency refugees, the central bankers can push their buttons all they want. No one will be on the other end taking their money and putting it to use. A mass exodus leaves the king with no one to rule.

"Governments like to believe they have some role in steering the economy through their central banks. If people can just turn on a dime and use their own currency, that severely limits the government's ability to do so," Gurri added.

The mere thought that people can flee their currency on a whim might be enough to force governments to think twice before devaluing their own paper bills. This nagging worry might also reduce a common problem: Politicians are addicted to using inflation as a means to reduce the real value of their government's debt to outsiders.

But it's time for a reality check. I left this aspect of Bitcoin last, because it's rife with all sorts of problems. The first deals with the effect this mass currency flight would have on the price and availability of bitcoins themselves. It's basic economics. What happens when there's a sudden, violent rise in demand? The price goes up. This is especially the case if we're talking about a relatively small, niche currency like Bitcoin.

Here's how the scenario might play out. The small, fictional country of Hyperinflatia starts experiencing—you guessed it—hyperinflation. Everyone there decides it's time to trade in their pesos for bitcoins. The world's Bitcoin exchanges all get hit simultaneously with millions of orders for bitcoins. It's a flood of willing buyers. Bitcoin owners willing to sell their bitcoins now see a market opportunity, and they naturally want to profit, so they raise their prices. Now, the citizens of Hyperinflatia are dealing with a double whammy. Their pesos are worth less, and bitcoins are worth even more. They might as well go for dollars, or euros, or something else that's widely traded.

The second problem with this idea is that this relocation of financial power is absolutely an antiauthoritarian revolution—and those currently at the helm won't sit idly by. To gauge what type of response we can expect from the U.S. government, I reached out to someone who's watched federal machinations up close for decades: Ron Paul. The congressman from Texas had just retired after 36 years in Washington, DC, where he had fought against every aspect of government intervention on currency. I asked him what the federal government would do if Americans started flocking to Bitcoin en masse to escape any future inflation.

"Governments absolutely demand a monopoly on money and credit. They're not going to give it up easily," Paul told me by phone. "If they lose control of interest rates—when that happens and they're trying to save the dollar—they're not going to want any competition. They're going to come down very, very hard. Just think of what we do to the various countries we don't like. We punish them with financial controls. We freeze their assets. They will do what they can to come down hard on it. Congress would get involved, because they can't stand the embarrassment if the dollar goes down in value."

Don't expect the government to wait until inflation kicks in, Paul warned. He expects lawmakers to first move on behalf of those with something to lose in the money game—banks, credit card companies, and transaction processors.

"Let's say all the forces in the credit card industry get annoyed, and they lobby. I don't doubt for a minute that special interests will come down like that," Paul said.

But what if—just for the sake of argument—that exodus does happen? Let's say people manage to buy bitcoins in secret. After all, even in places with strict currency controls, there's a lively black market for dollars. What then?

"It'll go down in history as the destroyer of the dollar," Paul said.

CHAPTER 7

The Case against Bitcoin

IT'S FAIR to call Bitcoin a startup currency. It has all the makings of a startup. Let's do a tally. It came out of nowhere; nothing like this existed before 2009. It's disruptive technology that will shake up our old, well-entrenched institutions. Its earliest adopters are tech-savvy folks driven by idealism. The whole system is maintained by a handful of computer coders.

Now for a healthy dose of realism: Three out of four startups fail.[1] Bootstrapped projects rarely make it off the ground, especially when they're perceived as principled crusades. Then there's the tricky task of getting people to buy what you're hawking. Make no mistake, Bitcoin is indeed peddling something: a totally new concept of money. It's a hard sell.

It all comes down to trust, convincing someone that this new version of money is at least as trustworthy and reliable as the physical coins and bills we're all so accustomed to. It demands confidence that the reward for your hard labor is safe. It's an epic battle. In one corner is physical money, used by humans for more than 5,000 years. In the other corner is money that exists only in the digital world and relies on the Internet, which for most people is less than 25 years old.

The conflict is daunting in its simplicity. People know how metal coins and paper bills work, how they look and feel. We're reminded of their power every day we buy our groceries, fill up our gas tanks, and pay for a movie ticket. And we trust them enough to give up most of our conscious lives to receive it as reward. A survey of those aged 25 to 54 showed that employed American parents spend 54 percent of their day at work.[2] We're all willing to toil away—in a steamy kitchen, an uptight office, a noisy classroom—as long as we're paid in physical money. We're not okay getting paid in bananas or books or video games. Why not? Because we're not under the delusion that those things can pay for rent.

That reveals two things. The first is that we're only willing to get paid in something that we know others will accept as payment. It's a feedback loop where you accept dollars because everyone else accepts dollars. This self-generated obstacle forms a major barrier for any new idea of currency, like Bitcoin. The second insight runs much deeper beneath the surface, and it's something most of us never question: our faith in our money.

British historian Niall Ferguson put this into perspective in his book, _The Ascent of Money_. Take a look at the back of a $10 bill. You'll find the phrase we all know so well: IN GOD WE TRUST. "But the person you are really trusting when you accept one of these in payment is the successor to the man on the front, Alexander Hamilton, the first secretary of the U.S. Treasury." Ferguson's point is that when you accept dollars for your goods or labor, you're trusting that the government won't get reckless printing money and make it worthless.

That trust quickly expands outward. You have faith that the U.S. president will safeguard the nation's currency. You trust that Congress will step in if things go wrong. Powerful business interests will keep bureaucrats from tanking the economy. Voters will replace them if necessary. American politics is accountable. The Constitution will be upheld. You believe the system works.

Bitcoin fails on every single one of these points. There is no expectation that businesses will let you buy from them with bitcoins. Rare is the person who's willing to get paid in bitcoins alone. There is no one to entrust with the fate of its value. There is no recourse if things go wrong. Perhaps most importantly, though, most people don't even know it exists. Less than half of Americans have ever heard of it, and only 13 percent of them trust it enough to prefer receiving bitcoins over gold.[3] From my everyday interactions with friends, family, and strangers, it's safe to say even fewer people understand it. Some of these things might change over time. But as of right now, Bitcoin is a poor competitor to the dollar we use today.

The fault is not in the software, but in ourselves. So far, the Bitcoin protocol has proven robust and secure. But huge barriers remain, because of how Bitcoin is perceived by the general public. They just don't trust it. People see Bitcoin's origins, its reliance on automated programming, and the very fact that its code is a freely accessible open-source project as weaknesses, causes for doubt. Are they being prudent and wise? Or petty and fearful? It actually doesn't matter. If they don't take a leap of faith, Bitcoin won't work.

I can count nine snags Bitcoin must overcome to make good on the promises I detailed in the previous chapter. None of these is particularly easy to solve, and I don't pretend to have the answers. But they're worth mentioning because something this groundbreaking and powerful deserves a skeptical look. Investors should hear warnings before they load their hard-earned savings onto a ship that's embarking on its maiden voyage. People who plan to start paying in electronic money have a duty go into this soberly. Businesses ought to know the dangers associated with the newfangled money they're about accept as payment.

The Origin Story

This is probably the worst. Are you really going to trade in your proven, working U.S. dollars sitting in a federally insured bank that's "backed by the full faith and credit of the United States" for a monetary system created by a faceless stranger? Bitcoin's creator decided to keep his identity hidden—at least up until the publishing of this book. It casts a shadow of doubt over the entire concept of Bitcoin.

Imagine if an architect secretly constructs a gorgeous, 10-story building, complete with Art Deco–style archways, horizontal banding on the façades, and a ziggurat pyramid roof. Then, on her own volition, she disappears. Do you pack up your stuff and move in? Do you feel safe doing it? How are you sure it's a safe structure? And wouldn't you wonder why she slid into the shadows? It's not just odd. It's highly suspect.

Satoshi Nakamoto's vanishing act doesn't exactly inspire confidence. I'll leave it to someone else to espouse at length on the reasons he decided to remain anonymous. Maybe he feared law enforcement would unjustly hunt him down. That's a valid worry. Or maybe he just wanted to distance something as incredible as Bitcoin from something as flawed as a human being. What if Nakamoto is actually an accomplished college mathematics professor who has served time for murder? Or what if he is a genius child living in the snowy mountains of the Yukon? Or how about a self-taught, stay-at-home mom? The world wouldn't take their currency experiments seriously. It sounds petty, but a clean record and college pedigree weighs heavily in real life. We humans are a dreadful bunch, quickly resorting to ad hominem attacks that focus more on judging the person producing the idea than gauging the validity of the concept itself. It reduces the value of others' creations, discoveries, and contributions. History has countless examples. Take the man who first proposed the existence of subatomic particles called quarks, George Zweig. As a young graduate student who had never published a single scientific paper, his inexperience was the very reason the research center where he worked, CERN, wouldn't publish his findings in 1968.[4] Perhaps Nakamoto feared a similar, baseless rejection. Whatever the motivations were, they suggest Nakamoto didn't have confidence that people would judge him fairly. If Nakamoto didn't trust the public, why should people be expected to trust Nakamoto's creation?

Nakamoto's disappearance doesn't help the case for Bitcoin. Here's an experience that served as a personal gut-check. On my way into the newsroom one morning, I tried explaining Bitcoin to my friend Gary Mcdonald, a security officer at CNN's New York offices. His first question was a doozy:

"So who's behind this? Who created this?"

As I explained Nakamoto and Bitcoin's mysterious beginnings, Gary's smile grew wider by the second. I stopped when I saw he could barely contain himself any longer.

"Naaaah," he said. "No way. You can't trust that."

On the other hand, anyone can figure out where U.S. dollar bills come from. The cotton-fiber paper notes are printed by the Bureau of Engraving and Printing. Larry R. Felix is in charge over there, if you must know. New bills are issued by the Federal Reserve, with Janet Yellen at the helm. These aren't people the average American can easily get on the phone, but at least we know their names.

The Empty Throne

The next snag for most people is the very thing that makes Bitcoin so innovative: It's a decentralized, peer-to-peer system. While that attracts free minds and free spirits, it repels the Average Joe who just wants to know someone is in charge.

After all, there's a benefit to concentrating power into a single person or team. They're motivated to perform well, because they'll be rewarded in money or reputation. There's punitive reinforcement too. When something goes wrong, they can be held accountable. There's no such thing with a peer-to-peer system. The protocol is in charge. Wait, so who is making sure this whole Bitcoin thing doesn't crash? That brings us to the next point.

Volunteers Run the Show

This will come as a surprise to anyone who isn't knee-deep in a technological field. Bitcoin is an open-source project, which means its software is wholly cared for by a community of developers who volunteer their time and expertise to scan the code for bugs, rewrite when necessary, and add improvements to the system. As an open-source project, anyone can see the source code, the blueprints that reveal all the magic—and potential mistakes to be exploited.

There's nothing inherently wrong with the open-source model. It works stupendously well for many of the tools we use today. The fact that anyone can read through the source code means that bugs are spotted faster and fixed more quickly than proprietary software that belongs to a single company and is heavily guarded. It also means that computer programmers from around the world can keep it up to date with the latest, niftiest technology, so open-source projects also tend to be more advanced and cutting-edge than their proprietary counterparts. There's a one-in-four chance you browse the Web with Mozilla Firefox, which is open source, and that works just fine. WordPress remains one of the world's top blogging platforms, used by more than 200 million websites. Linux is a computer operating system that runs on thousands of machines across the globe, everything from home computers to the U.S. Navy's nuclear submarine fleet.[5] Another is OpenSSL, the software most often used to encrypt the communication you have online with your email, social media, and bank.

But open-source projects have a flaw. If they're mismanaged or underfunded, the whole thing can crash—and no one's to blame. No one owns the project. It's a labor of love. Our experience with the security software OpenSSL serves as a warning. It was behind an event in early 2014 that shook the Internet for a few days. A few computer researchers looking through OpenSSL's code on their own discovered a massive, gaping security hole. The program that was on servers at major websites had a "heartbeat" function that pinged your computer to make sure it was still there. The problem? Outsiders who weren't supposed to read your encrypted conversation with a website could use that ping to tap into a computer's memory. If using OpenSSL is the equivalent of enciphering letters before sending them by mail, this was like leaving a window open that lets anyone peer in as you read the letter. It defeats the purpose. This "Heartbleed" bug had been inadvertently placed into the OpenSSL code two years prior and had quietly undermined more than 66 percent of major websites. Security experts I spoke to at the time called it the worst Internet bug ever. The OpenSSL Software Foundation raced to patch it, quickly sent fixes to the millions of devices and websites that relied on it, and everyone hoped no one had secretly exploited it. But on April 15, the Canadian Mounted Police arrested a

19-year-old who, they say, used the Heartbleed bug to hack into the country's tax agency and steal the Social Insurance Numbers of 900 taxpayers. The episode forced the country to delay its tax-filing deadline by nearly a week. How did something so pivotal to the infrastructure of the Internet—our communication, our finances, our safety—end up with such a massive flaw? OpenSSL is maintained by a handful of volunteers. Only four are considered "core programmers." The organization's president, Steve Marquess, would later tell me that, altogether, the team of volunteers contributes the work of three full-timers. This is the dark side of open source: being underfunded and understaffed.

During that ordeal, I spoke to Marc Gaffan, who cofounded the cloud security provider Incapsula. He said the Heartbleed incident showed how open-source projects leave no one to blame for a mistake. There's no liability. No one is culpable. But the point here isn't that open source should give up culprits for us to condemn; it's that this is what you get with volunteer projects.

"What do you expect? You got this for free. You get what you pay for," he said.

And that's how Bitcoin is currently maintained. Bitcoin's core developers are extremely talented individuals who love the project. Their involvement is about benevolence, not personal gain. They pour their hearts and souls into it. There's nothing categorically improper about what they're doing. Gavin Andresen, Pieter Wuille, Nils Schneider, Jeff Garzik, Wladimir J. van der Laan, and Gregory Maxwell all care deeply about this project. Otherwise, they would be spending their free time doing other things. But it will be a challenge to convince everyday people to adopt a leaderless currency kept alive by passionate volunteers.

Beware Deadly Bugs

This one comes up a lot, especially among tech-savvy folks who would love Bitcoin—if it weren't for their constant fear of software flaws. Bitcoin is purely a software play. It's all it is and all it ever will be. The software makes it powerful, but if there is even a tiny glitch, the whole system could come crashing down. This is a weakness you can't ignore.

It's not the same in the physical realm. A single, miniature mistake at the Federal Reserve won't suddenly wipe out the savings accounts at every bank. The cash under your mattress won't burst into flames. It would take a concerted effort by several people at the Federal Reserve and U.S. Treasury to seriously hurt the dollar. And it wouldn't happen in the blink of an eye. These kinds of things happen to the beat of a steady drum—even if it rumbles quietly in the background. Red flags go up. Disaster can be averted.

I can hear the counterarguments rolling in. Airplanes rely on digital systems, but we fly in them without a second thought. Our cars have more than 50 microprocessors in them, and key systems run on software. It's gotten to the point that folks in the auto industry tell me there's a joke engineers share at Toyota: The only reason they put wheels on a car is to not scratch the bottom of the computer chassis. But most people don't think about that. Tell them something runs entirely on software, and they immediately think about how many times Internet Explorer crashes on them. They remember all those times their banking app shut down halfway through a transfer.

The OpenSSL Heartbleed bug, which forced everyone everywhere to change their passwords, showed what a tiny coding mistake can do. There's no telling what kind of damage a software glitch can do to the Bitcoin system.

It's All on You

You should see the horror on people's faces when I tell them you can actually lose your bitcoins with a single click. Just delete the private key to your digital wallet. Misplace that, and you'll never get it back. After all, it's just a file. It's no different than an mp3.

By cutting banks out of the equation, Bitcoin empowers individuals. But it also shifts the entire responsibility of keeping that money safe to you. Consider that a digital wallet isn't just a wallet. It's also an account. There's a difference. If you're anything like the average person, you keep just enough money to get you by in your wallet, but you keep most of your money in the bank. It's not because it's more convenient to carry less cash. You do it because it's unsafe to walk around with hundreds or thousands of dollars at a time. Yet Bitcoin is more like having a collection of wallets. You keep some key pairs on you, others at home. You can keep your private keys stored in an offline device. But your private keys are not locked behind a fortified institution where your money is insured by the Federal Deposit Insurance Corporation. That's where banks have a real advantage over bitcoins. If someone robs a bank, they take the bank's money, not yours. If someone makes off with your bitcoins, you're out of luck. No one is going to pay you back. This is a turnoff to all but the most bold.

François Velde, a senior economist at the Federal Reserve Bank of Chicago, made this point in an essay he wrote about Bitcoin in 2013.[6] "Although some of the enthusiasm for Bitcoin is driven by a distrust of state-issued currency, it is hard to imagine a world where the main currency is based on an extremely complex code understood by only a few and controlled by even fewer; without accountability, arbitration, or recourse."

He continued: "Bitcoin is free of the power of the state, but it is also outside the protection of the state."

It's not easy to steal someone's bitcoins. The system's tight security is designed to prevent that very thing from happening. But that's a double-edged sword. If you misplace your digital wallet's private key or forget the passphrase that gave you access, your stash of bitcoins is as good as gone. It takes a brave person to take on the responsibility of safeguarding your own money and know that you are the first and last line of defense. Just ask James Howells, the British man who chucked out a hard drive containing the private keys of 7,500 bitcoins (when they were worthless). When the price of a bitcoin reached $1,000, his old drive was worth $7.5 million. But it was too late to get it back from the city dump.[7]

The lesson here is that Bitcoin isn't for the faint-hearted, or the irresponsible, or those who would rather sit back and let others guard their money for them. You need to understand how the system works, know how to use a computer, and be familiar enough with technology to recognize when you're making a bad decision. Maneuvering through the tech world is only easy if you know how to properly avoid bad turns into dangerous alleys. If you fall for a phishing scam by opening an email and clicking on a bad link, you could download a virus that secretly scans your computer for access to your Bitcoin wallet.

Most of us have gotten past this kind of worry in the modern world. Our money is safe at a bank, and we don't have to think twice about it. Even if you keep your cash under the mattress, you can still tell when someone has physically broken into your home. It's not as easy on a computer. You can't always tell if your digital door has been unlocked. A hacker could have tunneled into your computer to spy on you and steal your bitcoins, and without diligent antivirus and malware updates, you probably wouldn't know.

Bitcoin is frequently described as a Wild West. It sure is. It takes true grit. There are bandits around every corner. Many so-called banks and exchanges are actually fly-by-night operations to whom you can't entrust your money. But hey, it's free roaming out there, pardner. Are you ready to saddle up your horse, slip that revolver into your holster, and ride out? If you're not the tech-savvy, adventurous type, Bitcoin isn't for you.

Copycat Coins

There's nothing to stop anyone from taking Bitcoin's openly available code and creating an identical digital currency. What if a few computer developers and economists get together and come up with a better Bitcoin? Let's say they make this New Bitcoin easier to use and give it nifty new features. Currently, so few people use bitcoins that the market for New Bitcoin could easily outnumber and overpower the old version. What then? The value of old bitcoins would most likely drop. People's savings would take a hit. Businesses would be disinclined to accept them as payment. Anyone who ditched dollars for bitcoins would feel foolish, because this drop in value would feel like the very inflation they sought to escape. Even a one-month, 10 percent drop—which is common in the Bitcoin world—would be worse than anything the U.S. dollar has experienced.

It seems ridiculous to just start your own electronic money. But that's already going on. There's Dogecoin, Litecoin, Isracoin, Zetacoin, Primecoin, Peercoin, and Auroracoin. Some of these are actually based on Bitcoin, and none of these has caught on. But there's nothing stopping a competitor from dethroning the king. There were many social media platforms that drew in millions of people—including the incredibly popular

MySpace—before Facebook appeared and wiped them all off the map.

This kind of head-to-head potential for total replacement doesn't exist in modern currencies. What stops this from happening right now in the physical realm with U.S. dollars is that it's illegal to create an identical system (massive printers, central bank, and all). Europeans use euros, and no one can come up with an identical version that could quickly be adopted by a population greater than the 740 million people in Europe. One could say the same for every nation. No matter what new currency pops up, it won't be a perfect competitor to Nigeria's naira or Yemen's rial or Egypt's pound. Any successful digital currency could be a direct competitor to Bitcoin.

There's significant incentive for starting a new, better Bitcoin. Those who got into Bitcoin early and collected or mined a few thousand of them became millionaires when the price hit $1,000 and they sold their stock. It only happened to a handful of people. But that set a precedent. It introduced the world to a get-rich-quick scheme that would have seemed impossible in the past. Can't get wealthy with money that already exists? Create your own!

This is why Warren Buffett, when asked about Bitcoin as a guest on CNBC, expressed reservations about its value. "You can replicate it a bunch of different ways," he said. "And the idea that it has some huge intrinsic value is just a joke in my view."[8]

This isn't an analysis that's reserved for Columbia MBAs and stock valuation geniuses either. Many times while introducing this to people unfamiliar with Bitcoin, this is their knee-jerk response: "So I guess I can create my own money?" The perception that a new version of Bitcoin can just pop up is discomforting—justifiably so.

Commodity vs. Currency

Bitcoin has an identity crisis. Some see it as a commodity like gold. Its usefulness as an investment is dependent upon its gaining value over time. The traditional investing rules apply: Buy low, sell high. There's also an understanding that prices might be volatile—they could wildly swing up and down—but overall there's an expectation its price will eventually increase. Contrast that with those who view it as a currency. To make it functional as money, it needs to hold a steady value so people and businesses feel comfortable trading with it. Prices need to be unwavering enough that merchants can calculate revenue stream and easily figure out how to apply sales tax.

It's difficult to have both of these happen at the same time. Speculative investors like shaky prices, because they can find opportunities to buy on a low day and take advantage of a peak day. To everyday users who want it as a currency, shaky prices complicate transactions. If you buy an espresso in bitcoins just as the price dips briefly, you'll overpay and regret it hours later. Similarly, long-term investors like continuous growth in value. But if that's expected, anyone using bitcoins as a currency would rather hold them instead of spend them. That's terrible for the Bitcoin economy, as this creates disincentive to use your money. It's essentially deflation, the opposite of inflation. Economic activity slows down, and the system starts tumbling into a downward spiral. It's not easy to escape. Japan's economy has been dealing with this for two decades, leaving top economists perplexed and policymakers feeling hopeless.

Andrew Schiff is an investment consultant at Euro Pacific Capital who thinks that deflation is Bitcoin's biggest hurdle. "Bitcoin is a great idea in terms of how the market can take back its own fate and take away the monopoly of currency issuance from central banks," he said. "But the kind of price appreciation you've seen in 2013 is incompatible with it being a currency."

Catherine Mann, an economics professor at Brandeis University, thinks the volatility alone will prevent Bitcoin from truly taking off. The problem is inherent in the fact that a bitcoin lacks a stable source of value. People generally agree what the price of gold is, or a U.S. dollar, or a ton of grain. That isn't true with an electronic token. "Absent an established underpinning, a stable value, Bitcoin won't be used the way it was intended—as a currency," she said. "The number of bitcoins you need to use in a transaction has varied from 100 to two. That highly volatile price undermines its use as a means of exchange."

Bitcoin's track record so far shows that it doesn't serve well as a currency or investment. It's too unstable. Its 9,775 percent growth rate in the year starting December 2012 wasn't just explosive—it was nuclear. But it fell nearly 50 percent two weeks later.

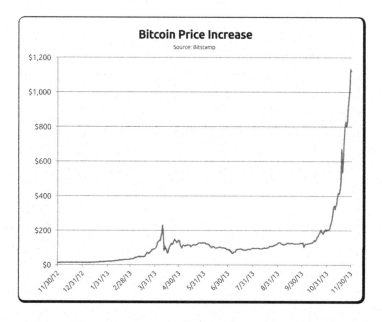

This shows how speculative it can be, which is good for neither long-term investors seeking it as a safe commodity nor casual users and businesses that need something steady to rely on for conducting transactions. This scares off newcomers.

It's Rebellious

We're not all activists, and most people are risk-averse. Bitcoin's best attributes are that it's groundbreaking technology that's individually liberating and inherently disruptive. That's not for everyone. Alternative money is also something of a political statement. It attempts to wrestle some control out of the government's hands.

Most mainstream economists, especially those in academia, agree that central banks have a place in our society to maneuver the economy. When I asked University of Michigan economics professor Miles Kimball about Bitcoin, his take was that the idea of a digital currency is great. But he's not a fan of an independent currency that's outside the control of the state. "It's unlikely governments will let go of monetary policy—nor should they," he said. "What Bitcoin does is that it really shows governments are behind the curve. Governments should be creating their own version of Bitcoin. Governments should be ashamed they haven't."

The same thinking applies for people who strictly agree with a political party. For American liberals, an independent currency threatens to upset their desire for a more robust government. Bigger schools, a wider welfare system, and increased government involvement in our lives costs money. While some of this money comes from increased taxes, the truth is that much of it comes from leveraging the national debt. But, as explained in the last chapter, the presence of a legitimate alternative money puts pressure on a government to be fiscally conservative (minimizing debt and avoiding inflation to keep that debt low).

For modern-day American conservatives, the same pressures apply. National debt is, in large part, what allows for sustained massive spending on the military and tax breaks for corporations and the rich. It would be more difficult to keep this up if an alternative currency exerts demands on the government to be more selective in its spending habits.

In that sense, Americans who fall squarely in either political party are correct in seeing Bitcoin as a hazard. This currency absolutely undermines the system. Traditionalists need not enter here.

Perfect Tracking

With all the talk about nameless digital wallets and nearly anonymous spending, this point gets lost on most people. However, as explained in the last chapter, Bitcoin's public ledger records every single transaction. If there's ever a law that mandates a person must register their digital wallet (as is expected), law enforcement now has the ability to track your every financial move.

This point was covered in the last chapter as a potential positive with Bitcoin and similar digital currencies. It is in the sense that it's great for building a case against a caught criminal. But for those who fear the growing, unwarranted mass surveillance of innocent people, Bitcoin only empowers government agents. It's no different than credit card transactions, which leave a detailed history, documenting how much you spent, where, and on what.

———

Much of this chapter reads like cynicism. It's not. This is the culmination of hundreds of conversations I've had with regular folks: new fathers, single mothers, retirees, college students, razor-sharp Wall Street traders, and wide-eyed teenagers. While all of them find Bitcoin and the idea of electronic money exciting and fascinating, each of them has expressed concern about at least one of the points I've listed. And they're right to be cagey about this. Money is not to be taken lightly. We've all earned our pay by laboring away for hours, giving up the precious time we could have spent with our families, friends, or ourselves. We're not just guarding our cash. We're fearful about turning entire days or weeks of our working lives into something wasted. It's natural to be distrustful about something that turns everything we know about money upside down.

James Rickards, a money expert who authored the book *Currency Wars: The Making of the Next Global Crisis*, summed it up best. Although he respects the technology that underpins the Bitcoin protocol, he can't take his mind off all the potential there is for things to go wrong. "There's technological risk, financial risk, legal risk, tax risk," he said. "What's the upside? I'd rather go to Las Vegas and play roulette, because I enjoy it."

There's no need to be fatalist about Bitcoin. None of the points made here necessarily sentences Bitcoin to death. But each of these will need to be addressed before a currency that's made of invisible ones and zeros overcomes our inhibitions and gains our confidence. Bitcoin's success depends entirely upon whether people believe. That gets at the very heart of the definition of money. A unit of exchange that no one trusts—be it gold, paper, or computer code—is nothing at all.

CHAPTER 8

The Rise and Fall of Mt.Gox

FOR A SECOND, Antoine Bourgouis felt as if he'd just won the lottery. The 34-year-old French executive living in Tokyo saw ¥100,000 pop into his bank account, and he could barely believe his eyes. It was money he feared he'd never see again. By all accounts, it might as well have dropped out of the sky in a neatly wrapped gift box. Bourgouis had gambled months earlier by dumping it on a glitch-ridden Bitcoin trading website. It had been so long since he'd heard back from the site's administrators that, for a while, it looked as good as gone. But there it was: $1,000 worth of cold hard cash.

It was February 25, 2014. Mt.Gox.com, once the world's No. 1 spot to buy and sell bitcoins, was now a blank white page. An estimated $400 million was gone. Thousands of trading accounts were suddenly rendered inaccessible, and they weren't just in bitcoins. Some were in euros, others in U.S or Australian dollars. Each ranged in size from a few bucks to entire college savings. Had the site been hacked? Was the company defunct? Did everyone's bitcoins just disappear in a flash?

Bourgouis was just as clueless as anyone else. But he knew he was among the few who made it out unscathed. His fellow traders were up in arms, groaning in public forums and talking to reporters about how they'd lost it all. In fact, given the fury, Bourgouis was better off keeping his head down. He had actually done better than survive. He prospered, receiving double what he'd originally put in.

Four months earlier, Bourgouis had transferred ¥50,000 to a newly opened Mt.Gox account. With it, he bought five bitcoins and watched them blast off like a rocket. But he couldn't stomach the daily price swings. Compared to the liquor and video-game penny stocks he'd traded a few years earlier—including one company that went bankrupt—this was madness. A bitcoin was going for $192 on Tuesday, then $200 on Wednesday, and back down to $175 on Thursday. The stress was too much. Bourgouis' appetite for risk was better suited for his day job, a conservative chief financial officer for a retail chain.

His five bitcoins doubled in value a few weeks later, and Bourgouis wasted no time selling them to another trader. But when he tried to cash out his ¥100,000, Mt.Gox administrators suddenly got pushy. They wanted proof Bourgouis was who he said he was. He provided everything they asked, and got nothing in return. He tried again in December. Then again in January. When it appeared in his bank account nearly 90 days after he'd requested it—a day after the site shut down—he didn't know how to explain it. But he was glad he pulled out in time.

"Thank God I did not buy again," he told me by phone. "With Bitcoin, I think I'm done. That was fun, it was interesting, but it was really a strong reminder that this is really pure speculation. There is no regulation, no guarantee, no safety net, nobody controlling what the numbers are. Even right now, nobody really knows if Mt.Gox was a big scam or really a security leak. It could just be another Ponzi scheme. Who knows where all the bitcoins went?"

How did it get this bad?

For all the cynicism that Mt.Gox was a house of cards waiting to collapse, the truth is, it actually was a house of cards. Magic cards, that is.

The website's first iteration was the brainchild of Jed McCaleb, a bright computer programmer obsessed with peer-to-peer networks.[1] He had created eDonkey 2000, which reigned as the top music-sharing site in the post-Napster era, and by 2006 he was looking for another disruptive project.[2] He came up with a novel concept: a website where card collectors could trade their decks like stocks. In this case, it would be players of Magic: The Gathering, a popular fantasy-themed trading card game that draws the Dungeons & Dragons crowd.

I could proceed with a thoughtful explanation of this eccentric game, in which cards showing breathtaking landscapes yield magical energy called "mana," which lets you cast spells with fanciful names like "lava axe" or "burning vengeance." I still keep a small collection around that I use as bookmarks, leftovers from my socially awkward middle-school years. But I digress.

McCaleb noticed that players were starting to migrate to an online version of Magic without any physical cards, and he thought a virtual trading floor would serve them well. He bought the domain MtGox.com and sometime in early 2007 launched Magic: The Gathering Online eXchange.[3] After a few months, it didn't catch on, so McCaleb abandoned the project and eventually turned the website into a place where he could advertise his next project, The Far Wilds, a video game of dueling knights and warring kingdoms.[4]

Then, in the summer of 2009, McCaleb heard about Bitcoin. He was fascinated with the liberating idea of an independent currency, but he couldn't find a decent place to buy them himself. That's when it clicked: Mt.Gox might be more useful here. He rebuilt the site as a place to trade bitcoins instead of Magic cards and launched it July 17, 2010. For a time, it ran solely on PayPal transactions.[5] The Bitcoin community was tiny in those days, so word spread quickly that it was eons ahead of its competitors. McCaleb advertised his site to Bitcoin enthusiasts, touting that it was always online, automated, faster, and easier to use. Users who kept their money on the website could keep buying and selling bitcoins at their leisure. He started off charging a 2 percent surcharge on every transaction and later dropped it to zero. But as the site gained in popularity and user demands started coming in, McCaleb became bored with the project. He never meant to become the administrator of a tiny stock market. And for a man who loves playing digital architect, the heart of the task was essentially complete. "It's not technically interesting," he would later say. And so, he looked for a buyer and found one in Japan: a young French fellow by the name of Mark Karpelès.

At that very moment, Karpelès was still getting used to his new home in Japan. But let's backtrack. The mild-mannered 25-year-old had spent years in Paris working for Internet companies and had long dreamed of moving to Tokyo. Like so many other computer geeks before him, he was drawn by an infatuation with Japanese culture and anime, the nation's unique animation style. When his employer, the e-commerce platform Nexway, finally agreed to let him work from abroad, he packed up his ginger-colored munchkin cat and a few hard drives, and left in a hurry. He documented every minute detail on his personal blog, from walks off the subway to baking apple tarts.[6] In those years, he was an open book. No one knew him, and he had nothing to fear. How that would change years later.

Back then, Karpelès was merely another cheery young man with entrepreneurial dreams—and a whimsical online persona. He was MagicalTux, PHP coding extraordinaire and a high-tech MacGyver who boasted he could save a broken Seagate hard disk armed with only "a business card, some wires, and a torx screwdriver." He spent much of that first year in Japan touring his new country, uploading videos on YouTube of train rides in the forest, street parades, and fireworks. A few months in, he finally got around to starting Tibanne Co., named after his feline companion. He used that as a platform to launch several web-related business ideas.[7] The first came in 2010 when he created Kalyhost.com, a service where others could host their own websites with guaranteed privacy. He set himself apart by being one of the first few businesses anywhere in the world to accept bitcoins as payment—at a time when they were going for pennies. Then came another Bitcoinerrific idea: smsZ.net, a text message service that would charge half a bitcoin for every Short Message Service sent worldwide.

Even as Karpelès tried to make himself a businessman, the fun-loving escapist kid inside him hadn't left. He spent his downtime immersing himself in the computer video game Minecraft—think Legos in an 8-bit world. There, he would hack away at pixelated blocks for hours. He'd dig deep into the digital dirt to mine for gold and iron ore. He constructed giant bridges that spanned across the blocky landscape. He built cyber citadels to his heart's delight.

But then another virtual fortress caught his eye: Mt.Gox. Its owner was no longer interested in keeping it running, and

Karpelès thought he could take it to the next level with smoother transactions and a better interface. He showed McCaleb his experience with web programming and system administration, and they reached an agreement, with the Frenchman buying 88 percent of Mt.Gox through his fledgling startup, Tibanne. On March 6, 2011, McCaleb announced he was passing the torch to MagicalTux, and the site's fate was sealed.

Facing growing demand from wannabe traders, Karpelès immediately started hiring technical staff—and paying them in bitcoins, of course. Meanwhile, he tried to keep up with the surge of customer money flowing his way by establishing bank relationships around the world. People had to send money to Mt.Gox to start trading, so the company was inundated in wire transfers. The service was clunky, and the initiation process was a bit of a hassle, but by most accounts, the small business of Tibanne was faring well. Karpelès charged a 0.65 percent fee on every transaction, and the volume was growing steadily.[8] Sure, he only made $1,000 or so that first month. But six months later, Mt.Gox would easily be raking in that much each day. Not bad for an automated service with a tiny staff.

He quickly realized the difficulty in running an exchange within the constraints of the Bitcoin system, though. "A trading system requires all the stuff that we do not know (yet) how to run decentralized," he wrote in a public post early on. One problem was figuring out a way to successfully deliver real-time, instantaneous transactions. The Bitcoin system doesn't verify them right away. Another issue was having the site serve as a responsible, trusted middleman in a system designed specifically to cut them out. These would be two problems that would haunt Mt.Gox until its collapse.

As if those headaches weren't enough, malicious bands of Internet trolls soon appeared. Karpelès was at the helm for only a month when Russian cyber bandits decided to flood Mt.Gox with illegitimate web traffic, performing what's called a Distributed Denial of Service attack (DDoS for short). The anonymous attacker demanded Karpelès pay a $7,000 ransom. Karpelès felt helpless as he watched his website get overwhelmed with malevolent computers sending him more than 6,000 connections every second, but he refused to give in. He took down the service for four days as he scrambled to find a new server and install some protective software. And while he did manage to bring the site back up with better defenses, the experience left newcomers with a bitter taste. Mt.Gox collected money like a mini bank, but the fact that it was still susceptible to a low-scale hack showed it wasn't ready for prime time.

As a safety measure, Karpelès would later say, Mt.Gox kept the vast majority of its clients' bitcoins offline, meaning that private keys weren't accessible via the Internet, so they were safe from hackers. "We always keep only 2 percent of the balance online, which means that even in the case something happens to the online coins we could still guarantee 98 percent of users," he said.

In some ways, though, hackers were the least of his problems. Karpelès was busy setting up companies around the world to gain legal permission to accept money from abroad, and financial firms weren't playing nice. One by one they shut out Mt.Gox, choking off the exchange's ability to receive incoming cash from abroad. In the spring, Karpelès struck a deal with an exchange in Australia, Technocash, only to have it fall through a few months later. It was the same in Hong Kong with HSBC, Karpelès announced online after he traveled there. "HSBC officially stated that they do not want to see anything related close or far to bitcoin, and kicked [us] out. We asked if it'd be possible to get back in and got politely told that it wouldn't happen anytime soon." Talks with banks in Canada were met with mixed results. Then Karpelès was blindsided when his longtime bank in France turned on him too. He took the matter to court, asserting his universal individual right under French law to access basic banking services.[9] One of the only venues that seemed to be working just fine was the American e-commerce company Dwolla (and even that would cause him problems soon enough). In the meantime, Karpelès met with lawyers and accountants to mitigate the situation everywhere, finding the financial world slowly shrinking all around him.

Meanwhile, the banks that did work with him didn't even play fair. There were complaints that wires sent to Mt.Gox were more expensive than originally promised. As it turns out, some were improperly charging fees under the assumption that they would have to convert currency to Japanese yen on the way to Mt.Gox's Tokyo headquarters, when Mt.Gox actually accepted all kinds of currencies. Padding each transaction with $30 or more caused customers grief, and Mt.Gox's public image took a beating in the process.

These quandaries couldn't have come at a worse time. Those pivotal first few months were the time when any entrepreneur should be keenly focused on growing the enterprise and establishing a sound business plan. But instead, the head of Mt.Gox was barely keeping his head above water, doing the equivalent of a doggy paddle to survive the tempestuous waves splashed by powerful banks clinging to the status quo. Add to that the surge in growth that simply outpaced what he and his tiny company could handle. From April to June 2011, the number of users on the site increased tenfold from 6,000 to 60,000. Users in the United States sent or withdrew $6.8 million over the Dwolla service in June alone.

All the while, Karpelès maintained a small frame of mind. As financial complexities swirled all around him, he retreated to the most minute of tasks. During two days in June 2011 when his exchange traded a quarter million bitcoins worth a combined $4.6 million, Karpelès sheepishly announced he had spent the last 48 hours manually checking nearly 1,000 of his frustrated customers' delayed pending transfers. It was starting to get out of control. When riled customers complained about a supposed hacked account and called for more security, Karpelès threw his hands up.

"Mt.Gox had a growth far too fast to give us enough time for this," he posted at a forum online.

Sure enough, in October the site got hit with another DDoS attack, with nefarious types flooding servers and slowing down service. Then came a major glitch, caused by a bug in Mt.Gox's software, that dumped sellers' ask orders and brought trade to a screeching halt. That was followed by yet another DDoS offensive that consumed all of Mt.Gox's computing power and locked out users. Karpelès assured customers there wasn't any data breach and bitcoins were safe and accounted for. When a fourth major DDoS attack slowed down trading again, Karpelès told users why he thought attackers were being so relentless.

"It is not a secret Mt.Gox is the largest Bitcoin exchange," he said. "Mt.Gox is an easy target for anyone that wants to hurt Bitcoin in general."

As Mt.Gox grew in popularity in 2012, Karpelès also made himself a key player in the way Bitcoin was perceived by political leaders around the world. That year, he helped form the Bitcoin Foundation and secured himself a prestigious spot alongside other Bitcoin entrepreneurs and academics. During that time, however, confidence in Mt.Gox began to erode. U.S. customers complained that withdrawals over Dwolla were delayed for weeks. When the company's European bank imposed daily transfer limits, wire transfers sometimes took two weeks or more. Business partners grumbled that Mt.Gox wasn't paying them on time. All of it was quite the antithesis to a digital currency system developed to cut third parties out of the picture. Karpelès admitted they were "working on improving the situation with liquidity," but provided few other details. The strangest kerfuffle occurred when Mt.Gox announced that it was expanding with full force in Canada and the United States via a new partnership with CoinLab, a Seattle-area startup with venture capital support—only to call the whole deal off.

Amid the chaos, customers noticed something curious was starting to develop as well. It was becoming harder to get your money back. Mt.Gox set caps on how much traders could cash out in a single day, limiting it to $1,000. Users who were willing to go through a verification process—and wait until Karpelès' tiny staff could process the request—got higher caps. But everyone was required to start providing photo identification, a utility bill, or other proof of address. Karpelès assured he was doing his best to operate within nebulous currency laws and abide by strict bank anti–money laundering regulations. But banks were dropping him anyway.

Still, the numbers kept ballooning. By March 2013, Mt.Gox was handling 2.2 million active Bitcoin wallets (and keeping an eye on another 18 million). It opened 60,000 new accounts that month. By April, it was creating 20,000 new accounts each day. A staff of 22 outside the Tokyo office worked furiously to verify accounts and deal with customers while a dozen in the office kept the website up and running.[10]

Then, unbeknownst to those trading on Mt.Gox, it blew up on May 9, 2013. That was the day U.S. Magistrate Judge Stephanie Gallagher signed off on a warrant allowing the federal government to quietly seize $2.1 million Mt.Gox kept in a Wells Fargo account.[11] It belonged to just another client with a vaguely important-sounding name: Mutum Sigillum LLC. But Shaun Bridges, special agent with the Secret Service, knew that was a subsidiary of the world's top Bitcoin exchange. The Secret Service alleged that Karpelès was operating his business illegally as an unlicensed money transmitter. The agent pointed to two questions Karpelès answered on a Wells Fargo bank account application form. One question asked, "Do you deal in or exchange currency for your customer?" The other said, "Does your business accept funds from customers and send the funds based on customers' instructions...?" The correct answer to both was obviously yes and would have required Karpelès to register with the Treasury Department and abide by strict know-your-customer rules. Karpelès said no.

The feds struck again the next week on May 14, when U.S. Magistrate Judge Susan Gauvey gave the green light for Homeland Security Investigations Special Agent Michael McFarland to seize another $2.9 million, this time at a little-known credit union in Iowa.[12] Few noticed when the feds raided Dwolla Account No. 812-649-1010, held at the Veridian Credit Union.

The third blow came as the CoinLab deal fell apart. The American firm sued Mt.Gox, seeking $75 million in damages. In response, Mt.Gox claimed CoinLab was unfairly withholding $5.3 million of Mt.Gox's customers' funds.[13]

All in all, Mt.Gox was out $10 million. News of this wouldn't appear until months later. But all three events were unseen explosions, like submarine-destroying depth charges dropped deep into the ocean abyss. Only bubbles appeared at the surface.

It suddenly became nearly impossible for traders to withdrawal their money from Mt.Gox, and no one knew why.

Customers were up in arms about what they perceived to be a liquidity problem, and they attempted what would amount to a run on the bank. But the withdrawals were painstakingly slow—to the point of arousing suspicion. Longtime clients began to tell incoming Bitcoin enthusiasts to stay away from the website entirely. A careful few listened. Daniel Weyer, a mechanical engineer for a Nebraska power company, heeded the advice he heard from others and went to a competing exchange instead. He would later tell me how fortunate he feels for jumping into this hobby late enough to know to steer clear of Mt.Gox.

But many more were like Alex Krusz. The web developer from Somerville, Massachusetts, thought the largest exchange in the world was naturally the place to be. Sometime in August, he pulled $500 from his bank account, walked into a CVS pharmacy store, picked up the red MoneyGram phone and listened as it autodialed the wire service's customer support line. He transferred all of it to Mt.Gox, bought five bitcoins and watched them soar in value in the coming weeks.

It began to unravel publicly in August 2013, when technology news websites discovered both federal seizures and raised the question of whether Mt.Gox—which had lost a combined $10 million—was actually insolvent.[14] It was worse than the startup just getting the wind knocked out of it. Losing that kind of cash would be a death knell for any small business, even one bolstered by longstanding and friendly bank relationships, insurance, and dedicated customers. By comparison, it seemed that Mt.Gox didn't stand a chance. Governments were clamping down on its financial network, and banks were kicking Karpelès by the wayside.

Landon King, a real estate IT specialist living near the Atlantic Coast in North Carolina, saw the writing on the wall.

He had been mining bitcoins for years with friends and had become intimately familiar with the technology and legality of the system. It didn't seem likely to him that the U.S. government would make such a bold move without reason.

"There were other exchanges that operate in the U.S., and the government didn't go after them. So I knew if the government was targeting a specific exchange, they were doing something shady. That turned me off," he said.

King fled from Mt.Gox the first chance he got. Instead of getting in line like everyone else to cash out his stash of bitcoins, he simply moved them over to CampBX, an exchange in Atlanta.

It wasn't so easy for Krusz. While he managed to transfer some of his bitcoins out, he wasn't able to get them all. Mt.Gox unexpectedly demanded he provide more proof he was actually himself and asked him to fill out a short questionnaire explaining how he'd use the money. Krusz found it bizarre and annoying, so he never got around to doing it. A part of him thought the whole thing would just cool off. But then there was that nagging thought in the back of his head. He'd noticed the site had a poor security record, and they hadn't been transparent about recent problems.

"I figured it was know-your-customer laws and regulatory pressure," he recalled. "But they may have known they had financial troubles waiting and they wanted to stall by making it harder to pull money out. There's no way for me to know."

By late 2013, the Karpelès who would frequently write to customers online and provide cheery, hopeful updates about the company had gone AWOL. Public announcements were brief and stiff. Clients clamored, but there was mostly silence on the other end. Mt.Gox was clearly in decline, with the lucky few who could pull their money out fleeing to competing online exchanges, like Slovenia's Bitstamp. And the captain who should have been at the helm of this sinking ship was instead preoccupying himself with a tiny pet project: his very own Bitcoin Café.[15] Like any frustrated professional who fantasizes about owning their own bakery in some quiet, idyllic Tuscan village, Karpelès had cooked up the wild idea of spending $1 million on a bitcoin-accepting French bistro on the first floor of Mt.Gox's Tokyo offices. For a while, the idea of launching it meant everything to him. His proudest achievement at the time? Hacking a cash register all by himself, insiders told *Wired* magazine. As the company bled money, customers, and professional relationships, Karpelès shifted his attention to tiny tasks he could master all by himself. He had once again retreated to minor distractions. Old habits die hard. Like any skilled computer programmer, he had a passion for building things. And when complex laws and bitter politics got in the way of the big dream, he created smaller ones that were absent all of that bureaucratic nonsense. It became painfully clear Karpelès had never stopped being the solo programmer more comfortable behind a computer screen than in front of a boardroom.

But even as things got worse for Mt.Gox, Bitcoin was on the rise. The price of a bitcoin went from $120 in October to $1,100 or so in December. Even to folks who'd never heard of this wacky online money, Bitcoin was starting to look like a lucrative proposition. And Mt.Gox was the apex of this hot new commodity.

It was around this time that I began to write to Karpelès and his staff repeatedly. He never called me back. It's only by looking back at the extensive digital footprint he left behind—in hundreds of online discussion forums, many of them since taken down—that I've been able to piece together what he thought, planned, and felt throughout this entire journey.

The big shakeup came on a Thursday evening, February 6, 2014. That's when, without warning, Mt.Gox halted all trading and froze every account. It had already been difficult to pull money out of Mt.Gox, but now you couldn't even use the website. The company sounded a major alarm, saying that there were serious problems with the way bitcoins were withdrawn from Mt.Gox wallets to external digital wallets. A fix was desperately needed. Was this another screw-up by the website? No, Mt.Gox said. It was much worse. This time, it was a problem with the bitcoin protocol itself.

Karpelès blamed a little-known software glitch dubbed "transaction malleability." Remember that all transactions have to be verified by the computers hooked up to the network. Each deal has a unique identifier, called a hash. Transactions are only set in stone on the block chain every 10 minutes. That leaves a rather large window for nefarious activity. Well, it turns out that you could submit two versions of a transaction—the right one and an exact copy with a falsified hash. Either one could get logged into the public ledger. For expediency, Mt.Gox processed customer withdrawals by relying on hashes—not the actual transaction itself on the block chain. Its internal records had fallen out of sync with the backbone of the Bitcoin system.

What could crooks do with this? They could pull money out of their Mt.Gox account and hurriedly send the Bitcoin network a forged copy. If the one with the fake hash made it into the block chain, they could then return to Mt.Gox and claim the exchange never sent the money. Please send it again, they'd ask. They'd point to the block chain and claim the deal never made it there. And Mt.Gox, only looking for the original hash, wouldn't realize the record was actually there. Mt.Gox would be duped into refunding the money. It's essentially receipt fraud, and it might have gone on for weeks, months, or even years. The tone in Mt.Gox's public explanation was ominous, calling the glitch a software bug that needed the attention of Bitcoin's small team of volunteer computer developers.

"The problem we have identified is not limited to Mt.Gox," it said in a press release. "Bitcoin transactions are subject to a design issue that has been largely ignored."

The shock sent the price of bitcoins plummeting around the world. Within a few days, peoples' bitcoins lost a quarter of their value, with bitcoins trading as low as $600. Mt.Gox had singlehandedly eroded faith in this technological experiment. After all, if the currency is nothing more than software, and the program is flawed, then what's the point?

Within days, however, it became clear the problem could have been avoided. Other exchanges had accounted for the glitch and programmed careful safety measures to work around it. And besides, in the real world, receipt fraud can only go so long until a retail store wises up and realizes it's issuing unreasonable refunds over and over again. Investors and businesses cried foul. Why hadn't Mt.Gox done the same? Karpelès promised customers he and his team were working furiously to disentangle the confusing knot in which they were tied up. They'd announce a fix soon and resume trading. Customers waited impatiently, nervously checking their accounts several times a day to see if trading would resume.

The first sign Karpelès wouldn't deliver on his promise came a few weeks later on a Sunday, when he abruptly resigned from the Bitcoin Foundation he helped create. Karpelès explained to his colleagues there that he had to bunker down and address his struggling startup, and they understood.

"Mt.Gox did the right thing to take care of business matters at hand," fellow board member Elizabeth Ploshay told me. "Mt.Gox has their hands full. They needed to handle what's going on with their exchange right now."

Competitors were less forgiving. The CEOs of six exchanges and digital wallet companies raced to reassure investors that the Bitcoin network was just fine.[16] Mt.Gox was merely a stain that needed to be wiped clean, they said. Bitstamp, Blockchain.info, BTC China, Circle, Coinbase, and Kraken issued a joint letter scolding Karpelès and laying out plans to "reestablish the trust squandered by the failings of Mt. Gox."

"This tragic violation of the trust of users of Mt.Gox was the result of one company's actions and does not reflect the resilience or value of bitcoin and the digital currency industry," the letter said. "As with any new industry, there are certain bad actors that need to be weeded out, and that is what we are seeing today. Mt.Gox has confirmed its issues in private discussions with other members of the bitcoin community."

The man who had shouldered much of Bitcoin's growth was now its No. 1 enemy.

A day after he quit the foundation, Karpelès took his website offline entirely. What was once the world's largest Bitcoin exchange became a blank, white page on February 24. He wiped the company's Twitter account too, deleting every tweet it ever sent. No explanation was given. Mt.Gox refused to speak to outsiders. Traders were stunned. Some even showed up in front of the company's Tokyo offices, holding up signs demanding to know how the bitcoins had disappeared.

But while the website might have been blank to the everyday person surfing the Web, a look at the website's code revealed something else:

```
 9      </script>
10      </head>
11      <body>
12          <!-- put announce for mtgox acq here -->
13      </body>
14  </html>
```

A Mt.Gox acquisition? What did it mean? It was anyone's guess. But at that very moment, a Bitcoin-trading blogger by the name of Ryan Selkis shared a document that had been sent to him anonymously. It was titled "Crisis Strategy Draft," and it read like a public relations pitch explaining how to clean up the company's tarnished image. But there was something else: damning information detailing the extent of the damage.

According to the document, Mt.Gox had lost 744,408 bitcoins—worth about $400 million at the time. The reason: the Internet-connected "hot wallet" had leaked, allowing someone to siphon out the contents of the extra-secure "cold storage."[17]

"The reality is that Mt.Gox can go bankrupt at any moment... with Bitcoin/crypto just recently gaining acceptance in the public eye, the likely damage in public perception to this class of technology could put it back 5–10 years," the document read. "This isn't about saving Mt.Gox anymore."

The purported plan: Shore up liabilities to investors, give Karpelès the boot, flee Japan, and rebrand as Gox. These were bold moves to avoid a bank run—the very kind Bitcoin was designed to get rid of.

Mt.Gox wouldn't say publicly whether the document was legitimate or not. However, there was at least one sign that lent it credibility: Just a day after Karpelès shut down Mt.Gox, he bought the website address Gox.com from a domain collector just outside Manchester, England. The seller, Andy Booth, wouldn't call me back, but the proof was there. I teamed up with a computer researcher at Berkeley and combed through the Internet registration records showing when they made the deal.[18]

There was more. The document claimed to reveal all of Mt. Gox's finances. If it was right, then the company had raked in $10.7 million in sales and $2 million in profit for the year starting on April 2013. Those are solid numbers—until you realize that the $10 million seized by the U.S. government and Coin-Lab had turned the entire business upside down, not to mention the $400 million lost in customers' funds.

Most traders who spoke to me voiced utter disappointment. They were in one of two camps: The Mt.Gox team improperly secured its clients' money, or stole it themselves. Either way, it became clear they had trusted their money to an outfit that didn't know how to properly handle it. Among them was Mickael Saladi, a 29-year-old in Miami who had kept four bitcoins with Mt.Gox and was sour about losing what was once worth $4,400. The lack of professionalism is what bothered him most. The least Mt.Gox could do is say what's going on, he told me. Instead, all he had was that empty white page.

Karpelès finally appeared in public that Friday, February 28. He ditched the usual T-shirt and jeans and showed up in a gray suit, a loosened tie around his neck. He was flanked by several lawyers as he sat down before a crowded room full of reporters. Dozens of cameras were pointed directly at him. The shy young man who moved halfway around the globe to launch a dream was about to crush it in one fell swoop. The company was filing for bankruptcy protection in Japanese court. Mt.Gox had lost 750,000 bitcoins, they explained—plus another 100,000 of the company's own stash. It amounted to nearly half a billion dollars. Hackers had somehow managed to pick the biggest Mt.Gox pocket of all, thanks to what Karpelès merely described as a "weakness in our system." The attorneys did most of the talking, but Karpelès issued the apology.

"We are working on it and, anyway, in the meantime, we are sorry for troubles caused by this," said an emotionally reserved Karpelès. "We had a problem with the system that caused a loss in bitcoins to our customers. We identified the problem, and we are working on this."

This was the situation Karpelès feared most. Years earlier, back when he just started managing this obscure website, Karpelès had promised its tiny group of users that he'd do his best to leverage it into the world's successful introduction to Bitcoin. Even then he was worried about the heavy burden on Mt.Gox to pull that off, warning them on a Bitcoin forum that "the immediate future of bitcoin is heavily reliant on the public and political perceptions of what we do, and how we do it." And yet here he was, surrounded by strangers with cameras asking accusatory questions about the failure on his watch. He had betrayed the trust of more than 100,000 people, and none of them had any recourse with their hard-earned money. How pleasant it would have been at that very moment to reverse time and be away from it all, back behind a computer, just MagicalTux chopping away at digital blocks and building pixelated castles in the sky.

Karpelès stood up, put his hands at his side, and lowered his head. Following the tradition of his new adopted home, he let out a long sigh, gave a deep bow of shame and held it. His heavy breathing was muted by the rapid-fire rat-tat-tats of snapping cameras that echoed in the tiny room. Mt.Gox was dead.

In the days that followed, something began to dawn on everyone. Bitcoin had evolved from an academic experiment limited to the world's tiny community of cryptographers to an economic powerhouse whose combined value was worth more than $5 billion in bitcoins alone. And yet the folks leading this monetary revolution were guys who would rather build compilers than companies. Mark Karpelès was only one example.

I reached out to Evan Rose in San Diego, who was starting his own Bitcoin ATM company at the time, Genesis, to see if he felt the same. After all, he was in his mid-twenties himself. He was more passionate about that point than anyone else.

"What we're seeing right now is the evolution of Bitcoin from amateur hour to professional money coming onboard," he said. "The people running the systems right now are not necessarily businessmen. For the most part, they're people who came into this project without grasping the value or risk of it. The ecosystem is maturing, but it's a little scary for everyone involved."

That point was especially apparent to those outside of the Bitcoin world. Peter Leeds, an analyst in Toronto who pays attention to speculative penny stocks, pointed out that Bitcoin is essentially going through growing pains. He compared it to the swell in technology startups in the late 1990s—and the crash that followed.

"If you look back at the dot-com bubble, people were running businesses, but they didn't know how to run a business. This is the same thing," he said. "A lot of the people getting involved with Bitcoin don't understand the complications behind it. They're getting involved too young, too early, and they're taking on a whole new concept that's bigger than them."

That became even more apparent when, shortly after filing for bankruptcy protection, Mt.Gox relaunched its website and allowed clients to log in and view their supposed account balance. Customers were quick to note that a static number on a screen means nothing. There's no telling where that money resides. There's no way to withdraw funds. There's no proof it's actually there.

Some thought it was like a bad joke, a feeble attempt to keep stringing them along. Jake Dearlove, a creative director at a London advertising agency, didn't think it was any better than a mirage. His 0.5024 BTC were as good as gone, he told me.

When I asked if he felt the $289 loss in any real way, he said it felt like more than that. After all, that was worth $550 just a few weeks before. "I'm actually quite annoyed," he said. "It does seem odd to me that they'd go through this effort to update us. Why would they? They must have some interest in keeping some kind of positive equity associated with the name."

It got even worse when Karpelès announced that, whoops, they'd found 200,000 of the lost bitcoins. It was in an old wallet they hadn't checked for months. Traders were beside themselves. What started as gross incompetence now reached comedic levels of stupidity. Nick French, a Colorado beekeeper who sells his honey for bitcoins, was appalled. Sure, he was still hopeful he'd one day see his 5 bitcoins again. But with every passing day—and subsequent Mt.Gox gaffe—his hope of getting back that $2,898 worth of bitcoins was fading.

"They have some serious problems. Two hundred thousand coins just show up somewhere? Come on. I don't believe it. What's next? They'll say it wasn't really 200,000, then pull it back? No. I don't trust them anymore. I don't know the whole story. I thought it was a hacking problem. Then there are reports of the CEO hiding the money. I don't know what to believe. But it's caused a lot of problems for a lot of people."

Weeks after I had spoken to French, Dearlove, and many others around the world, a Tokyo court blocked Mt.Gox's attempt to restart its business through a bankruptcy. A court-appointed administrator, bankruptcy trustee attorney Nobuaki Kobayashi, announced that Karpelès would be investigated to see if he was liable for the exchange's failure. The company was set on a course for liquidation—essentially a meltdown where no one gets any money back. Meanwhile, a class-action lawsuit involving an estimated 50,000 rattled Mt.Gox clients claiming more than $200 million in losses waited in the wings, with lead attorney Jay Edelson saying that liquidation "would be a disaster for customers." Whatever the company's fate is, it won't be easy on anyone.

For all of its failures, though, the fall of Mt.Gox is merely the tale of a business gone belly-up. Karpelès' actions turned out disastrous, but at least his intentions seemed good-natured and sincere. And those who traded on the site merely wanted to buy and sell these new, fun tokens. It wasn't a wretched hive of scum and villainy. That role belonged to an underground empire few had ever heard of before 2013: Silk Road.

CHAPTER 9

The Dark Side of Bitcoin

THE BIGGEST hit to the Bitcoin-fueled online black market came on a Tuesday afternoon, October 1, 2013, on the quiet second floor of a small library in San Francisco. A pale, thin man sat at a corner table near the science fiction section, typing away at his laptop. It was Ross Ulbricht, a computer-savvy 29-year-old from Austin, Texas, who was living with a couple of roommates just a few blocks away. Court documents would later allege that this one man commanded Silk Road, the largest criminal bazaar on the Internet—all from his computer. But at the moment, Ulbricht was chatting online with someone who, unbeknownst to him, had secretly been talking to law enforcement. It was 3:15 PM, and Ulbricht was unaware that half a dozen FBI agents were closing in on him. They were in plainclothes as they slid past rows of books and beige walls. When they finally reached him, the agents grabbed him and pinned him against a floor-to-ceiling window overlooking Diamond Street.[1] The agents quickly seized his computer on the assumption that it housed evidence of a vast, illegal empire and access to 26,000 bitcoins belonging to Silk Road customers.[2] That same day, the FBI took control of the Silk Road website and shut it down. For the thriving online community of druggies, thieves, hackers, and assassins, it was the end of a lawless escapade. For the rest of us, it was a moment of awakening. The criminal underworld had found a new way to do business: Bitcoin.

In the days that followed, Bitcoin's image took a brutal lashing. Few had ever heard of the digital currency, and now it was being paraded as the go-to money for illegal activities. That view wasn't unfounded. The shutdown of Silk Road provided a unique view into the inner workings of a massive black market—and Bitcoin's place in it.

The website that launched in early 2011 was essentially an illegal eBay, allowing independent vendors to post their wares. Buyers made purchases through the website, which played a role as the middleman connecting them both. But what made it notable was its rapid success. To date, the most revealing details about Silk Road come from a 33-page FBI document requesting Ulbricht's arrest warrant.[3] In its first two years or so, the website had brokered 1.2 million illegal deals worth 9.5 million BTC and claimed a commission of 614,305 BTC. Those statistics meant that a single online black-market kingpin had amassed 5 percent of all bitcoins in the world at the time. But what made this a more incredible feat is that it was essentially the meteoric rise of a black market startup. Here's how this dark eBay's numbers translate into 2014 dollars: It had brokered $4.1 billion in deals and raked in $266 million in revenue. It had 3,877 vendors selling to 146,946 people around the globe. What made it all possible was Bitcoin's pseudo-anonymity.

Online black markets were around before Silk Road. They too relied on virtual money that was difficult to trace back. There was Costa Rica–based Liberty Reserve, which received anonymous wire transfers and offered electronic tokens in return. Another was E-Gold, which provided gold-backed digital dollars. Both became go-to currencies for trading drugs, weapons, and child pornography.[4] But the U.S. government was able to shut them down in 2007 and 2013, because they were centralized monetary systems.[5] Bitcoin, by comparison, has no single entity that can shut it down. Users of Liberty Reserve and E-Gold migrated to bitcoins, and Silk Road became their home.

Silk Road couldn't be accessed with any old Web browser, because it only existed on the Tor network, the Internet-within-an-Internet that masks the location of all computers that are connected to it. (It's a great tool for keeping political dissidents safe, but it does the same for criminals.) That offered one layer of anonymity, because you could visit the website without anyone knowing the location of your computer. But Bitcoin changed the game. Buyers could make purchases without ever knowing who was selling them the drugs. Sellers would mail vacuum-sealed packages of cocaine, heroin, or LSD to strange addresses and remain clueless as to who paid them. Bitcoin's nameless digital wallets were a part of it, but the Silk Road website had developed an added layer of secrecy. The website temporarily held the money in a deal in escrow. Why? It had developed an internal bank, called a "Bitcoin tumbler," to make it difficult to trace any transaction from Wallet A to Wallet B.

Silk Road's "Bitcoin Tumbler"

It would send all payments through a series of dummy transactions, bouncing a bitcoin around several times, before heading to its true destination. For providing buyers and sellers that security—as well as a one-stop shop for everything illegal—the website charged a rate between 8 percent and 15 percent.

The marketplace attracted all types of outlaws from every corner of the world. Most of the site was made up of simple drug dealers peddling cocaine, heroin, LSD, marijuana, psychedelic mushrooms, and high-end pharmaceuticals. But there was so much more. A "forgeries" section offered fake passports, driver's licenses, Social Security cards, credit card statements, car insurance records, and utility bills. Hackers listed their services and offered to break into Facebook, Twitter, and email accounts. They sold computer viruses, password-stealing software, and other types of destructive malware. There were tutorials on hacking ATM machines. Some even sold contact lists of professional hitmen.

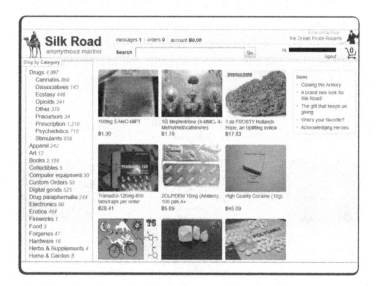

The website's vocal and eccentric founder was a mysterious figure who called himself Dread Pirate Roberts, a reference to the William Goldman novel/film *The Princess Bride*. He coordinated with vendors, resolved disputes, and assured everyone that the website's design and use of bitcoins would keep their identities secret. That's why in 2013, when a vendor named Friendly-Chemist tried to extort him out of $500,000 and threatened to publish the names of several vendors and customers, Dread Pirate Roberts did what anyone in charge of a black market would do. He tracked down what he thought was FriendlyChemist's true identity—a married father of three living just outside Vancouver, Canada—and coordinated with another Silk Road vendor to have him killed. Dread Pirate Roberts paid 1,670 bitcoins to have the job done and demanded a photograph of the man's body. He got what he wanted. These secret conversations—along with all of the website's internal records—were revealed when the FBI tracked down a computer server that kept the site running. That's what led them to website administrators and eventually to Ulbricht himself.

In the months since his arrest, Ulbricht has not commented publicly about his detention. He faces charges that he conspired to launder money, traffic drugs, hack computers, and played the role of a criminal enterprise kingpin. In February 2014, he pleaded not guilty in a Manhattan court. His lawyer in New York, Joshua L. Dratel, has since asked for the case to be dismissed, arguing that Ulbricht was nothing more than a "digital landlord" whose website simply became a haven for criminals.[6] Federal prosecutors are fighting that portrayal.

However, the fall of Silk Road did not bring an end to Bitcoin black markets. Just a month after Silk Road was shut down, a nearly identical website calling itself "Silk Road 2.0" appeared on the Tor network, led by another mysterioso also calling himself the Dread Pirate Roberts—just as the *Princess Bride* character was a series of different people all claiming to be the same pirate. Buyers and sellers flocked to this revived version, and continued doing business as usual. The website served as a middleman between buyers and sellers, temporarily holding on to funds in its own accounts during a deal. Buyers would put their bitcoins into Silk Road 2.0's accounts, and sellers would withdraw them. This iteration didn't last long, though. Within a few months, the website claimed it was hacked and lost 4,440 bitcoins it held in escrow for its users. The explanation didn't add up, so clients cried foul and accused the site's administers of faking the hack and stealing the money themselves. Because the entire thing was illegal, there wasn't any legal recourse for anyone. The episode served as yet another example of how Bitcoin—by design—doesn't work well with shady middlemen. All transactions are irreversible, and anyone with access to your digital wallet can empty it forever. But the numbers don't reflect a grand awakening. By April 2014, Silk Road 2.0 had grown even larger than its predecessor, offering 13,648 listings for drugs, weapons, hacking tools, and a myriad of illegal services.[7]

Bitcoin's peer-to-peer system doesn't limit it to big, Amazon-style illegal marketplaces, however. Individual stores have popped up all over the place, and perusing through their wares shows how Bitcoin has truly become the currency of the underworld. Slow, costly and potentially identifiable wire transfers are a poor second choice to speedy Bitcoin transactions.

There are countless computer hackers willing to work on a freelance basis, as long as they're paid in bitcoins. Here are the going rates at one solo operation called "Rent-a-Hacker": Want to hack someone's email or Facebook accounts? It'll cost you 0.64 bitcoins. Need a website taken down or have someone's computer spied on? That'll be 1.6 bitcoins. And the description of the services (complete with spelling and grammatical errors):

Ill do anything for money, im not a pussy :) if you want me to destroy some bussiness or a persons life, ill do it! Ruining your opponents, bussiness or private persons you dont like, i can ruin them financially and or get them arrested, whatever you like. If you want someone to get known as a child porn user, no problem.

At a website called "Arms International," pistols and AK-47 prices are listed in U.S. dollars, but the seller only accepts bitcoins. A payment worth $725 gets you a Glock 17 pistol and 100 rounds of 9mm ammunition. An AK-47 made in Romania fetches $560, and that includes a complimentary gift: enough bullets for just over three magazines. Another is BMG, short for Black Market Guns, which carries a wide selection of semiautomatic rifles, fully automatic submachine guns, and more. All its prices are listed in bitcoins, and it claims to ship overnight FedEx within the United States.

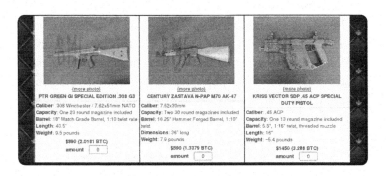

A website known as the "ccPal Store" sells access to stolen financial data in bulk. A package of 100 PayPal or eBay accounts goes for 0.23 bitcoins. The same number of credit cards will cost you 0.34 bitcoins. Another seller who runs "PrePaidBliss" hawks debit cards loaded with $700 to $1,000. A group that calls itself "Tor ATM Skimmers" markets hardware that can be installed at an ATM machine and spies on unsuspecting bank customers. The tiny camera will be $2,000 and the vendor only accepts bitcoins. "Onion Identity Services" claims it can get you a fake British passport—that will somehow match up with the government's own databases—for just over 12 BTC. For the same price, you can get fake driver's licenses in Denmark, the Netherlands, and Norway. All products ship free from Germany. Those who produce child pornography pay 0.02 bitcoins a month to use a service called "The Matrix image uploader," which stores their pictures and allows them to share them on secret forums and members-only websites.

And to top it all off, a service that calls itself "The Coin Cleanser" claims it can launder your dirty bitcoins, because it partners with legitimate brick-and-mortar businesses and can make it seem as if the money was spent legally. Sure, it could be a total scam meant to steal your bitcoins. But it's worth noting this isn't the only service of its kind.

This is the type of elusive criminal behavior that law enforcement currently faces. It helps explain why the U.S. Department of Homeland Security told the Senate committee that oversees its activities that the agency is taking "an aggressive posture" toward illegal use of virtual currencies. Here's what DHS official Brian de Vallance wrote to senators on November 13, 2013:

> The most critical capability for transnational organized crime is to quickly and quietly move large quantities of money across borders. The anonymity of cyberspace affords a unique opportunity for criminal organizations to launder huge sums of money undetected.

To fight this sort of thing, the FBI in early 2012 partnered with other federal agencies to create a group solely dedicated to Virtual Currency Emerging Threats, or VCET. And it's why the Financial Crimes Enforcement Network, the Treasury Department bureau that monitors money laundering and terrorist financing, has clamped down on Bitcoin exchanges. Trading platforms like Mt.Gox are required to register as licensed "money services businesses," just like their competitors in the money transferring industry, such as MoneyGram. This requires exchanges to file documents proving that they know who their customers are. It's an attempt to chip away at the namelessness of Bitcoin wallets.

Those rules are already being used to chase after laundering with Bitcoin money. An alleged connection to Silk Road is what took down one of the top Bitcoin exchanges in New York City, BitInstant, at the start of 2014. The black market website Silk Road only dealt in bitcoins, which provided a lucrative opportunity to anyone selling bitcoins there. According to federal investigators, a 52-year-old Florida man by the name of Robert Faiella made a business of providing bitcoins to Silk Road customers. Under the alias BTCKing, Faiella sold them more than $1 million worth of bitcoins. Faiella, in turn, was getting all of his bitcoins from BitInstant—with the permission of its CEO, Charlie Shrem. Investigators said Shrem knew that Faiella was involved in the black market but never tipped off the feds—even as Faiella was exchanging more than $20,000 a week for his Silk Road clients. Shrem was arrested at John F. Kennedy International Airport and charged with operating his startup as an unlicensed money transmitting business. His company instantly went belly-up. Two of his largest investors, twin brothers Cameron and Tyler Winklevoss, distanced themselves from him, as did the Bitcoin Foundation where Shrem was vice chairman. Shrem denied the charges and has publicly called it an attempt by the banking industry to flex its muscle on the Bitcoin community.

But there's a simpler explanation. As Ernie Allen, president of the International Centre for Missing and Exploited Children, said when he testified before the U.S. Senate in 2013: "The attractiveness of Tor and Bitcoin...is based upon a perception of anonymity...thus, if the perception of anonymity diminishes, we believe the criminal use will diminish with it."

Not all governments are approaching Bitcoin with reasonable intentions to shut down criminal networks, though. Most have no idea what it is.

CHAPTER 10

How Governments Are Responding

THE LEGAL WORLD of Bitcoin has often been described as a new frontier. And it's not just Bitcoin, but all other virtual currencies that run independent of established and regulated banks. Entrepreneurs with grand ideas about new ways to trade them—whether it's on investment exchanges or neat wallets that run on your smartphone—all venture into a barren landscape where it's rarely clear if you're operating legally or not.

For every story of a successful Bitcoin startup on the verge of striking it rich, there's another that went down amid questionable circumstances or is under criminal investigation. Just as digital payments company Circle Internet Financial announced it had received $17 million from venture capitalists, Charlie Shrem sat at home contemplating his recent arrest and the disappearance of his virtual wallet startup BitInstant.

For the most part, governments have refrained from giving their blessings to money that competes with their own—quite the opposite. They paint them as dangerous and unreliable, with some going so far as to characterize them as predatory moneymaking schemes.

But most countries have not actually outlawed them. As of early 2014, only Iceland and Vietnam had gone that far. The most forward-thinking countries have held back from shutting enterprises down, because they see the potential to become hubs of innovation. Others have refrained from taking a militaristic approach for fear of sending their entire digital currency economy into the shadows. But in every country, the story is the same. This new technology has skipped ahead of the laws on the books, and politicians are trying to catch up.

In most cases, lawmakers are struggling to understand it. Who can blame them? The idea of computerized coins that you can't see or touch redefines many aspects of what we're accustomed to calling money. Add to that the fact that the creation of new bitcoins is totally out of a government's control, and you can see how politicians are inclined to reject it.

Spain makes a great example. Legislators there are grappling with the fact that Bitcoin operates as a network, a currency, and a commodity all at once. The government is interpreting it as a piece of property, because its Civil Code uses that term to describe valuable objects that change hands. But this particular law doesn't quite fit this new-fangled digitized dollar. After all, it was written at a time when Spain's spectacular technological achievement was an overweight steamboat cruiser called the *Reina Regente* that soon sank and cost the lives of 420 sailors.

"It's curious, but it's true: In Spain, Bitcoin is regulated by a law made in 1889," Pablo Fernández Burgueño told me. He's a tech-savvy attorney in Madrid who's made it his personal mission to educate lawmakers on how best to treat Bitcoin and other virtual currencies.

"Bitcoin is legal in Europe. The problem we find is that the laws we have to use are very old. Our goal now is to come together and agree on how we should interpret these laws," Fernández Burgueño said.

What results is a slow awakening, in which the smartest governments tiptoe forward with narrow legal guidance, occasionally offering tax rules here and money regulations there. The last thing they want is to create black markets or skew people's incentives the wrong way.

For all the criticism the United States government gets on this, the feds haven't yet taken the hostile approach so many Bitcoin enthusiasts have been clamoring about for years. During the first few months of 2013, the news headlines were dominated with apocalyptic quips claiming Bitcoin was doomed for this or that reason. Many journalists were in an unannounced race to write Bitcoin's obituary, citing an angry congressman or drastic IRS rules. But the clampdown everyone feared? It hasn't happened yet.

That is, at least as of this writing. The United States is suffering from the same problem facing every other government: The laws don't quite match up with this new technology. They're not starting from scratch, though. Some general rules apply.

First and foremost, bitcoins have value. It's evident because people can get richer or poorer with them. That means they can be taxed.

Second, certain goods are restricted or illegal, no matter how you acquire them. It's unlawful to buy a brick of high-grade cocaine that just made its way across the Caribbean Ocean in a go-fast boat. Despite people's ignorance about gun laws, only a handful of licensed folks can actually acquire a machine gun. Money laundering is wrong. Digital currencies don't let you scurry around these prohibitions.

Third, we've granted government the role of consumer protector, so it hunts down instances of fraud. While people are free to gamble on speculative investments—like the complex and dangerous financial instruments known as credit default swaps—they can't be lied to about those assets. People can't be duped into a Ponzi scheme that promises business profits but actually pays out investors with the money it gets from new, incoming investors.

This gives most nations a starting point for devising new rules. As we'll see, some have already started down that path.

———————————————

In the United States, the most elucidating guidance came from the taxman in March.[1] The IRS issued a formal notice saying that Bitcoin transactions are taxable. It also clarified that it would treat all digital money as property, not currency.

That has major implications, and understanding them is a bit complicated. But we'll piece this apart and use frequent examples. For reference, I consulted with several tax lawyers, as well as some former and current IRS folks.

> **EXAMPLE BOX 1:**
>
> *Let's assume you're a mechanic and your friend makes custom guitars. Her car needs serious work that would put her back $1,000 in labor, but she's short on cash. Both of you are willing to make an even trade. You fix her car, and she makes you a rebuilt Fender Stratocaster that wails like a banshee. In real life, you would have to calculate the value of that guitar and pay taxes on it. It's an aspect of taxes that most people don't know—or willfully ignore.*

The first thing to note is how this applies to everyday people who get paid in bitcoins. The simplest aspect is that payments made in Bitcoin worth $600 or more are treated like transactions made with property. Those kinds of deals already exist today.

This rule applies to any kind of Bitcoin payment worth $600-plus. If you're a business owner who pays workers with bitcoins, those payments need to go on the federal W-2 tax forms you hand them every year. They now have to pay federal income tax on it. After all, it is income in a literal sense. It's the same if you pay independent contractors in bitcoins. You must include the payments on their 1099 forms, so they can declare it as income.

For the same reason, this is also applicable to miners who use their computers to generate bitcoins, because they get rewarded for their work. The federal government thinks of them as self-employed entrepreneurs.

Now the question on everyone's mind is: What's the value of a bitcoin anyway? The IRS says it's the "fair market value." In other words, whatever the going rate of a bitcoin was the day it was earned. It seems like taxpayers may rely on any bitcoin exchange for that price. The IRS didn't name a specific exchange and with good reason. Exchanges are private, and there's no assurance any exchange is operating legally—or will stay open forever.

Making matters more difficult, the value of a bitcoin fluctuates every few seconds. It can swing $10 in any direction on an average day. This is where it's suddenly important that the IRS says bitcoin isn't a currency. It's not just semantics. The IRS has a special exemption for what it officially recognizes as "currencies," so you don't have to deal with this when you travel abroad and enjoy a slightly stronger euro. Not so for Bitcoin. Every fluctuation matters.

EXAMPLE BOX 2:

Imagine buying a bitcoin for $500. The trading price goes up, and it doubles in value. Now you spend it all on a brand new keyboard that retails at 1 BTC ($1,000). You technically experienced a $500 gain. You have to report that on your next tax return.

The law, as prescribed, forces people to keep track of the value of a bitcoin when they got it and when they spend it. To do this, a Bitcoin user must keep a strict record of every purchase made all year long. Each payment requires this calculation:

Gain = current bitcoin value – base bitcoin value

It's easy to see why this can quickly get annoying. Every time you buy a cup of coffee, you have to jot down all the details.

As if this doesn't complicate things enough, there's something else. Remember that you have to track the gains on your bitcoins. If you buy them separately, you have to track the gains on each bitcoin. This is a predicament for any Bitcoin user, because it creates bitcoin discrimination. One bitcoin is better to spend than another. This is a concept that Georgetown Law professor Adam Levitin explained on the academic blog Credit Slips. For a currency to work, all units of that currency must be completely fungible. That is, they're each identical. In U.S.

dollars, one $10 bill is as good as any other $10. It doesn't matter when you put Alexander Hamilton's face into your wallet or when you pulled him out. If bitcoins aren't fungible, they don't work as a currency.[2]

> **EXAMPLE BOX 3:**
> *You buy bitcoin A for $500. The trading price skyrockets and reaches $1,000. You buy another, bitcoin B, at $1,000. You decide to buy a guitar amplifier that retails 1 BTC ($1,000). But wait, it matters which bitcoin you use. If you spend bitcoin B, you experienced no gain. There's no reason to report to the IRS. But if you spend bitcoin A, you experienced a $500 gain in value. You owe taxes.*

For some of the reasons mentioned already, the Tax Foundation think tank in Washington, DC, said the IRS made a bad call.[3] "They completely miss the primary use of Bitcoin, as a currency for both transactions and wages. The tax treatment and compliance requirements as part of this notice are inappropriate for that usage of virtual currencies," the Foundation said in an announcement.

Is it really that bad? In theory, yes. Even the IRS knows that. As someone at the agency (who spoke on condition of anonymity) told me, "I wouldn't want that headache. Someone could say we set the bar too high."

But that's exactly why the casual user buying Bellinis with bitcoins won't see the IRS on their tail. The U.S. tax authorities gave Bitcoin users a task that's nearly impossible to comply with, and they'll have limited ability to enforce their own laws. Digital wallets are difficult to trace to actual individuals. Besides, as former IRS commissioner Mark Everson reminds me, the agency is strapped for resources.

Everson, who's now an executive at the tax consulting firm alliantgroup, said the IRS will probably have a hard time following up on those rules. There are two things the IRS does— interpret the law and administer it—and it isn't easy to go through with step number two, he said. But the agency doesn't have a choice. When I asked if the IRS rules are merely a revenue grab or an attempt to hobble Bitcoin, he said it's neither. It's the agency's job to clarify what the tax standards are. "What they couldn't afford to do is allow bitcoins to become a vehicle to escape taxation," Everson said.

He's right about that. No currency can be allowed to become a safe haven for tax cheats and miscreants; not in a country with a functioning economy, anyway. What the IRS rules really do is provide the U.S. government with more ammunition to go after the black market and big currency traders who dodge taxes. Much the same way that it was tax evasion—not Prohibition violations or violence—that put Al Capone behind bars for seven years, the federal authorities can now crack down on people spending bitcoins on drugs, assassins, and computer viruses by focusing on the tax cheating aspect of it instead of the actual misdeed.

"The IRS doesn't have the tools to find the little guys. But now the IRS has huge tools to leverage against criminals," said Steven Rosenthal, a senior fellow with the Tax Policy Center.

The last thing that's worth noting about taxes in the United States is that the IRS, by classifying bitcoins as property, has paved the way for states or local governments to impose taxes on them too. Sales taxes might apply whenever someone acquires a bitcoin. That means any business that sells bitcoins would have to charge a markup for them.

Marc Nickel, a Silicon Valley attorney who closely studies Bitcoin, said this isn't a far-off possibility. Most big states have caught up with technology and now tax digital goods. A software distributor who sells a $100 program from a district where there's a 5 percent sales tax owes her local government $5. The same would apply to anyone selling bitcoins, or even a fraction of one.

EXAMPLE BOX 4:

Here's why a business that accepts bitcoins should trade them in for dollars right away. Let's say Eddie's Banjo Boutique sells one of its twangy instruments for 1 BTC (valued at $500). Then the price of a bitcoin drops to $400. Eddie suffered a loss. But he's about to get kicked while he's down. He still owes sales tax on $500, not $400. He can't pass the buck on to his local government.

It all sounds disastrous until you realize bitcoins are difficult to track to actual people. And, as the IRS reminds me, this isn't too different from cash in that we have a voluntary tax compliance system. It relies on honesty. Do you really think the owner of that tiny, cash-only convenience store is reporting all of its income? During my two years reporting on U.S. small businesses, the answer I got from entrepreneurs was a resounding no.

What would it take for the IRS to track everyone? Tying people to specific digital wallets the second they buy bitcoins from online exchanges. Alex Daley, a technology investment analyst with Casey Research, suggests that the IRS could simply apply to exchanges the same rules that already exist at brokerages. Those financial institutions have a legal obligation to keep track of investors and submit information about their clients to the federal government. These know-your-customer laws allow the IRS to keep track of people's investment gains—and what they owe on taxes.

"If they make that requirement and hold bitcoin exchanges to the same standard as brokerages, you can no longer be anonymous with Bitcoin," Daley said.

As it turns out, more strict regulation on Bitcoin exchanges is on the horizon.

———

There exists a Bitcoin Bogeyman. He's in the nightmares of Bitcoin's most devoted followers, a specter whose coming has been foretold ever since the first batch of bitcoins was mined. He's a bumbling old man who doesn't understand computers and never cared to learn. He wears an ill-fitting pinstripe suit to his mundane public sector job. He's quick to judge and doesn't listen. He's beholden to the powerful banks that put him in power. He's a man with a government-issued hammer, and every disruptive financial innovation looks like a nail. He's the one who's going to kill digital currencies the first chance he gets. He's a regulator.

On the first pleasant day of spring in April, I decided to visit the government official best positioned to fill that role. I hopped on a subway from CNN's offices at the corner of Central Park and rode it to the last stop on the southern edge of Manhattan. There, surrounded by offices belonging to hedge funds and trading floors, was the base of operations for New York's Department of Financial Services (DFS). Somewhere inside 1 State Street was Benjamin Lawsky, the state's first superintendent of financial services.

Lawsky and his brigade have an outsized role for what turns out to be a modest outfit. DFS is made up of 1,000 or so employees working on nine floors, and their task is gargantuan when you consider this is a state agency charged with keeping an eye on the financial capital of the world. Consider that there are 27 sectors under their watch. There are some 675,000 folks working in the financial sector.[4] Goldman Sachs alone has a staff of nearly 33,000.[5] New York Governor Andrew Cuomo created the agency in 2011 to consolidate the state's Insurance and Banking Departments, some of the oldest such regulators in the nation. In the aftermath of the financial crisis, it became clear that a single entity should oversee the increasingly complex (and risky) assortment of financial products, especially as the lines get blurry between commercial banks, investment banks, and insurers. Lawsky's job is to make sure he catches the fuse next time it's lit—before the whole system blows up again.

I waited for the superintendent inside the 19th floor's empty boardroom overlooking the harbor, watching the same helicopter buzz around the Statue of Liberty every few minutes. The door popped open behind me, and in walked the state's top financial regulator flanked by his press secretary. He was energetic, athletic, and cheerful. And in a well-tailored suit no less. We sat down, and he wasted no time deflecting the skepticism about his intentions.

"Bitcoins...provide a potentially very powerful new technology that, as it develops into the future, could serve as an important alternative payment system that people can use," he said. "But we have to study something we really didn't have a lot of background in. What is this? Money transmission? Is it here to stay? To decide how to regulate it appropriately, we have to come to grips with what it is we're regulating. And in a way that puts the protections you need into place—consumer protection, safety and soundness of financial institutions, anti–money laundering—without squelching it and killing it.

"You don't want to make the use of this technology so burdensome or unwieldy that the technology can't develop."

He's adamant that he's not here to bring progress to a screeching halt. The IRS rules seemed, to him, heavy-handed.

"What I hope to happen is we will have a set of common-sense regulations that'll allow digital currencies to develop. And five or 10 years from now they will become better and more useful and popular with people. It's never going to replace fiat currency—I think that will be unreasonable to expect—but it will be an alternative payment system people use in certain circumstances to make their online financial lives more convenient, more effective, more efficient."

Bogeyman be damned. But let's backtrack a bit to something more fundamental. I posed the question that had been dogging me for months.

"So, is bitcoin money?" I asked.

Lawsky took a deep breath, leaned back in his chair, and ran his hand down the length of his tie. "Is Bitcoin money? I think Bitcoin—I'm not going to answer the question," he chuckled. "It's obviously being used as something of value. I'd have to think about how one defines money. I try not to get too deep into the semantic fight."

He'd rather leave that to politicians and the IRS, he said. But we got into a discussion about modern money anyway. How much money do you currently have in your bank account that you've actually held? It's just a number on a computer screen. My bank doesn't actually transport stacks of paper bills in a truck whenever I transfer money into a friend's bank account.

"Absolutely not, it's just pressing a key," Lawsky said, tapping the desk. "So is it really that different?"

To this regulator, digital currencies also provide a great opportunity. While some politicians have only warned about the dark side of intangible computerized tokens, Lawsky has been thinking about how law enforcement can benefit from the block chain's permanent record of every Bitcoin transaction. He can't help it. He's a former federal prosecutor who's constantly on the tail of money-laundering suspects and shady bankers, and chasing them in the current world of money isn't easy.

"Look, I deal with a lot of these cases of international money laundering with wire stripping. It's a herculean burden to try and do what we call lookbacks and figure out what took place over a five-year period: The number of transactions, the information's been stripped out. And it takes years and years to put these cases together and figure out what actually happened."

Currently, investigators sift through hundreds of thousands of paper or electronic documents that could have been doctored. It's a messy process that inevitably erupts with one side claiming proof of covered-up wrongdoing, and the other side screaming false charges. Those circumstances put Lawsky in a difficult spot a few years ago, when he brought a case against the London-based banking behemoth Standard Chartered.[6] His investigators were sure the bank had violated U.S. sanctions against Iran by allowing money from there to funnel through offices in New York. They accused the bank of going rogue, instituting a policy to conceal the identities of Iranian clients by "stripping" documents of key information whenever their money moved from offshore accounts into Manhattan then back out again.

An estimated $250 billion made that illegal U-turn over a decade, Lawsky's investigators alleged. But consider this: The bank's New York branch cleared an average of $190 billion in U.S. dollar transactions per day. Bank regulators said they spotted 60,000 unlawful transactions, but think of how complicated it was to separate those from the millions of others.

The bank eventually agreed to pay $340 million in civil penalties to settle the money-laundering charges. But not before rejecting the accusations and attempting to tarnish Lawsky's name. He came under fire for going it alone, with some calling it a career-defining, politically motivated maneuver or just pure American hubris of telling a British bank what to do.[7]

How much easier would it have been if investigators could point to an immutable public ledger of transactions, a permanent map to trace every monetary move ever made? There's potential there, Lawsky told me. It won't come as a surprise that Lawsky is interested in the immutability of digital record keeping—that is, if it can't be hacked. But Lawsky is equally enthusiastic about a digital currency's ability to hide a buyer's identity in the private sector. He recognizes the value in hiding who you are from the growing army of information-gobbling retailers, social media providers, and communication companies that sell our most personal details to credit bureaus and data brokers.

How do you enjoy both sides of that coin, traceability and anonymity? That's where Lawsky's regulatory framework kicks in. At the time of our sit-down interview, his team was still devising rules. But his thinking was: License the exchanges where people first create a wallet and buy a bitcoin. Then let users roam free from there.

"What's really potentially exciting about digital currencies is...you can envision a world in which when you enter the bitcoin ecosystem, you've got to identify yourself," he said. "But once the ledger has that, you could be able to move around the ecosystem largely anonymously. It's almost the best of both worlds. Law enforcement knows that it can go and track that down if something nefarious happens. But people who want privacy online as they engage in transactions potentially get it."

With all this cryptotalk, I wondered aloud if he understood the underlying mathematical algorithms and computer code that enable the system to work. His answer was point-blank: no. But he felt comfortable relying on a dozen regulators and lawyers who have talked to computer scientists, Bitcoin miners, investors—heck, even the Winklevoss brothers—to get it right.

Plus, he leverages the youngest staff in the office, people in their late twenties who give him a more tech-savvy perspective on things. They even convinced him to stage an Ask-Me-Anything session on the public bulletin board website Reddit, in which he thoughtfully answered questions about his intentions and asked a few questions back. The outreach earned him some credibility, and a stranger in the crowd even tipped him a tiny fraction of a bitcoin, worth about five bucks. A month later he still hadn't retrieved it, because he didn't know what to do with it—or whether it was even legal to take it, he told me. But he is considering buying a portion of a bitcoin on his own and ordering something off Overstock.com.

He's not in a rush, though. Lawsky doesn't think the concept of a virtual currency is going to disappear anytime soon, especially when the banking world's high transfer fees make it an industry ripe for disruption. The cost of sending money abroad is exorbitant, he said. It's about time that changes. But he wants to play a careful umpire and not side too heavily with the bankers he currently keeps in line—or the techie revolutionaries at the gate.

"There's this tightly regulated, slow world of banking colliding with what has been this unregulated, very fast moving, innovating, changing world of technology," Lawsky said, punching his fists together. "And what do you do with that collision?"

If you slam newcomers with the same rules as the established powers, you'll probably kill the innovation, Lawsky surmised. "But if you just let the tech side run wild and innovate, you won't have sufficient protections and end up with a Mt.Gox."

And that, he admitted, is his biggest fear. What keeps him up at night are the dangers lurking in the blind spots, the ticking time bomb he needs to catch before it explodes. When he started his tenure in 2011, European markets were on the verge of imploding. There was talk of default in Greece, Ireland, Portugal, and Spain, threats that bond holders everywhere would have to take a haircut, receiving a fraction of the money they lent these governments. Even though Manhattan is 5,000 miles west of Athens, it would still experience the fallout as if it were an epicenter of its own. Lawsky oversees 100 foreign bank branches, and most had exposure of some sort. Every week or so, Lawsky met with his capital markets division, and the team would go over an "emerging risks report." They kept a close eye on interest rates, bond sales, government statements—always praying they wouldn't miss a thing. The oncoming wave of digital currencies is much smaller in scale, but the thinking is the same.

Assume, he told me, that there are a few major virtual currency exchanges in New York City. "If we become overconfident or complacent that we know everything in this constantly changing, evolving, innovative world of technology, we could miss something significant. What I would never want to see is...that there was something we missed and an exchange collapsed. We're going to work very hard on our blind spots so we put protections in place—that may seem overly conservative to some—to make sure we don't have a collapse.

"The key is to never think you know everything, and never think it's under control; and always be worried, which is not a fun way to live your life. But that's what you do as a regulator."

———

The United States deserves some credit for being proactive. Right now, only a few other countries are issuing clear guidance on taxes. Finland's taxing authority is trying a tactic similar to its U.S. counterparts, collecting on capital gains whenever a virtual currency appreciates in value. Ireland is considering the same. Others are still trying to figure out how to define digital money so that it's taxable but doesn't give the impression they're vouching for its authenticity.

The following section gives a brief overview of how governments are responding. Be advised, because virtual currencies are so new, the laws of different countries are currently in flux, so it's difficult to keep track of all 196 or so. But it's worth talking about the measures some of them have taken so far. I give kudos to the Law Library of Congress for scouring through government statements and news reports and the tiny team of volunteers at BitLegal.net that keeps track of recent changes.

You'll notice one entire continent that is conspicuously absent: Africa. That's because, by most accounts, Bitcoin is still relatively unknown there. The M-PESA system already in place dominates the landscape, and at the present time, competing systems of currency are a hard sell for a region that's practically bankless for the majority of people there.

Europe

We start with Europe, a relatively rich continent where 61 percent of its 816 million inhabitants have Internet access.[8] That makes it fertile ground for virtual currencies. Electronic money operates in a legal gray area, because the European Union in 2009 declared that e-money can't be legal tender—but that doesn't make it illegal.

Only Germany has made the leap forward to recognize Bitcoin, giving it tacit approval. The country's financial regulator, BaFin (*Bundesanstalt für Finanzdienstleistungsaufsicht*), issued a statement in late 2013 saying bitcoins are units of account, and therefore legally binding financial instruments. It didn't go as far as calling them legal tender, but BaFin acknowledged that they have value. It went easy on regulation, though, adding that people who create the currency don't have to get bank licenses.

Finland, Slovenia, and the United Kingdom have been mulling over ways to tax it. The tax authority in Finland, Vero Skatt, has taken an approach that's similar to the United States. It applies capital gains taxes whenever a virtual currency is swapped for another currency. Users are also taxed on the appreciated value of an electronic token. They can't deduct their losses, though. Slovenia's position is that bitcoin isn't a financial instrument, but it still has the ability to tax it—although how isn't clear. The British government has clearly stated that bitcoin is unregulated. But its taxing arm, Her Majesty's Revenue and Customs, has classified bitcoins as "single purpose vouchers," allowing them to be taxed between 10 percent and 20 percent. That's a major markup, and many worry this could choke off bitcoin use in the UK.

On the other end of the spectrum is Iceland, where the government has found a novel way to freeze digital currencies before they blossom. Its people are prohibited from sending

Icelandic krónur abroad to acquire bitcoins, so unless they mine them at home, they can't get their hands on them.[9] That restricts the inflow of digital currency, making it unpractical to use. The world of cypherpunks produced a predictable, knee-jerk response: A mysterious programmer appeared from the ether under the name Baldur Friggjar Odinsson, becoming Iceland's own Satoshi Nakamoto.[10] He used Iceland's public national database to tally each of the country's 320,000 people, and in March allowed each one to claim 31.8 Auroracoins. It was a dud.

Russia has also taken an aggressive stance against electronic money, but it hasn't gone as far as a clampdown. In early 2014, Russia's top prosecutor affirmed that the ruble is the only official currency. It said anonymous payment systems are money substitutes and therefore illegal. It singled out Bitcoin and said people and businesses can't use them.[11] Shortly thereafter, however, the country's central bank chimed in and called the clampdown premature. An immediate ban isn't necessary, it said. The main goal is to protect citizens from fraud and prevent money laundering and tax evasion, it said. The country's frenetic response might sound unwarranted, but the Russian government is looking out for its national coinage, which is in trouble. In the years since the global financial crisis, Russians have been experiencing stagflation—a bitter brew of inflation and an economic slump. To get a better grip on lowering that inflation, the Bank of Russia has plans to weaken its currency controls and allow the ruble to float freely in 2015.[12] There's a major downside to having the ruble fluctuate naturally and value itself at whatever it trades for on the foreign exchange market. The rubles sitting in Russian banks' vaults will drop in value, and so will the market capitalization of those banks. In short, Russian authorities are reluctant to let alternative electronic money become safe havens for people fleeing the ruble.

Every other government in Europe has taken a hands-off approach, for better or worse. The Belgian finance minister doesn't think government intervention is necessary. Denmark's financial supervisor said it won't regulate Bitcoin, and it won't tax personal transactions either.[13] The Bank de France has warned about the dangers of mingling with virtual currencies, and the government might soon take a closer look at requiring licenses of exchanges. Ireland's revenue commissioners are devising ways to tax bitcoins, but the Irish Parliament has said it doesn't regulate them. In the Netherlands, the president has likened bitcoin to "tulip mania," and the finance minister has said bitcoins can't be seen as electronic money. Poland's finance minister refuses to recognize bitcoins as legal currency but said they're not illegal. Italy has followed the European Union, which is to say it hasn't done much at all. Most other governments have stayed mum.

Mattia Gottardi blames what he calls a European political class that's totally out of the loop on the latest tech. He's an Italian attorney who lives in a small mountain town that borders the Alps, where he keeps a close eye on laws about virtual money. He reckoned that if he were to ask 100 members of the Italian Parliament how to classify Bitcoin, 99 would be clueless. It's a dangerous ignorance, because the lack of clear laws allows for players to unfairly warp the value of virtual currencies, avoid paying taxes, and launder money. "The industry is still totally devoid of rules, thereby favoring distortions and poor security," he said.

One final government in Europe is worth a mention, if only for its oddball scheme. Alderney, the northernmost of the

Channel Islands between France and Great Britain, is a tiny place. You'd probably miss it if you were looking at the average map. But it has grand Bitcoin plans. The government is playing with the thought of minting and issuing physical tokens, and filling vaults with them.[14] It's hard to take this seriously, considering that one of Bitcoin's strengths is the ease with which someone can pay using some awful fraction like 0.00531 BTC without batting an eye. Then again, this comes from a place that often describes itself as "two thousand alcoholics clinging to a rock."

The Americas
When it comes to alternative payment systems, the Americas are unique. The region has been experimenting with electronic money for more than a decade, so there's something of an appetite for it. But its laws are no more developed than elsewhere.

Canada has not imposed rules treating Bitcoin differently than any other currency and is handling the matter with a light touch. The government's accounting investigators charged with tracking terrorist financing decided in 2013 that Bitcoin exchanges aren't subject to the same sort of tight scrutiny as banks. The Canadian Revenue Agency expects people to pay barter taxes when they spend their bitcoins on goods and investment taxes when they sell them as a commodity.[15] More striking, however, is the government's willingness to protect consumers when something happens to their virtual money. Unlike the many law enforcement agencies that stood idly by after the Mt.Gox collapse, Canadian police launched an investigation after Flexcoin, a Bitcoin bank in Alberta, was supposedly hacked and robbed of $600,000.[16]

Meanwhile, Mexico instituted anti-Bitcoin measures that serve as a roundabout way to quash its use.[17] Its central bank prevents licensed financial institutions from using it or processing transactions, creating a major obstruction for exchanges, which need to process incoming funds from traders.

The region's socialist bloc—Cuba, Ecuador, Nicaragua, Uruguay, and Venezuela—has said little about Bitcoin, but that's due to the fact that it's already well underway with its own electronic currency, the sucre. The system is largely an experiment for the time being, but the bloc is hoping that it will reduce their region's use of the U.S. dollar in business transactions—and push the United States' imperialist influence out of South America.

Most other governments have said nothing, or merely issued boilerplate warnings about volatility. Colombia reminded its citizens that nothing but the Colombian peso is legal tender.[18] Brazil's banking authority said it doesn't yet present any risk to the nation's financial system.[19]

Andrés Chomczyk, an attorney in the Argentinean capital of Buenos Aires, told me that Bitcoin's tiny presence in the region hasn't yet merited the attention of nearby governments. "Until it gains more international traction, I think South America will remain silent on Bitcoin," he said.

Then there's Chile, where a small group of Libertarians with an anarchist bent has taken that silence as a license to explore an oddball escapist project: the creation of a free market paradise that runs entirely on Bitcoin.[20] The isolated village is called Galt's Gulch, named after the main character in Ayn Rand's *Atlas Shrugged*, the lengthy book about rational selfishness. It's the brainchild of Ken Johnson, a California real estate agent who bought 15 acres nestled in a breathtaking valley between Chile's capital and the west coast. He's marketing 430 lots as an independent haven for the free-thinking, hardworking types

Rand spoke about in her book, the ones who disappeared when the world's socialist leeches asked too much of them. For you video-game enthusiasts out there, don't be surprised if this immediately reminds you of the best critique against Rand to date: the underwater enclave of Rapture presented in the video game BioShock. For those who don't know it, it's worth reading up on.

Asia

Asia is another hotbed of activity, because it's extremely populous, coming of age economically, and its connectivity to the Internet is pervasive. And unlike in Europe, countries there are constantly swapping all kinds of currencies. Hong Kong, Singapore, and Taiwan each have their own dollar. There's the Japanese yen, Thai baht, Malaysian ringgit, Philippine peso, and South Korean won. And let's not forget the two major players: China with its renminbi (better known by its basic unit, the yuan) and the rupees of India.

The nastiest response so far has come from Vietnam, where the communist government has barred citizens from trading bitcoins and declared electronic currencies illegal.[21] Its central bank cited virtual currency connections to money laundering and other crimes. There were various reports of online exchanges starting there anyway, despite government warnings that operating there wouldn't be permitted.

Singapore, on the other hand, took the business-friendly road we've all come to expect of the emerging entrepreneurial hub. It laid out a plan for regulating business entities, like currency exchanges, requiring them to know their customers. The move was narrow, confined to a single purpose: prevent money laundering and terrorist financing. It also set a tax policy that goes easy on investors. Anyone who gets paid for work in bitcoins must dish out income taxes. But capital gains aren't taxed at all.[22]

One would have expected robust regulation in Japan after the Mt.Gox debacle, but the country has been slow to move. Japan's hands-off strategy is essentially being non-communicative. Its government has said Bitcoin isn't a currency, but in the years that it was home to the largest exchange in the world, it never moved forward on enlightening guidance. Banking laws there say lenders can't set up digital wallets for customers or manage transactions. At the same time, laws don't prevent others from managing bitcoins.[23]

China is the government with the most aggressive anti-Bitcoin stance in the region that hasn't formally illegalized it. Like Mexico, it's found a roundabout way to clamp down on the currency. Banks and payment companies can't mingle with the currency, and that includes clearing transactions and making trades. That cuts off the role banks play as backend processors, the way they work with credit cards. It also prevents exchanges from having any bank accounts to store the incoming cash. In fact, the value of bitcoins took a nosedive when the People's Bank of China specifically ordered banks to close the accounts of nearly a dozen exchanges in a matter of weeks. Why the stiff shoulder? Some have commented that China is in a similar position to Russia in that it maintains a strict control of its currency, the yuan. Here's how tight that grip is: As of 2013, it didn't even allow traders to buy yuan at more than 1 percent above or below its central bank rate. Its government isn't too keen on a competitor—even a tiny one—that could shake things up. So, in response, it handles Bitcoin like deadly, radioactive waste. It isn't the first time the country has taken a hardline stance with a virtual currency, though. When QQ Messenger, the country's most popular messaging app (with 800 million users) embedded its own virtual money in 2009, China's central bank issued a guidance saying that trading QQ Coin was illegal.[24]

India is only slightly less hostile. Federal officers raided a prominent exchange, BuySellBitCo.in, and the company promptly shut down.[25] The problem, it seemed, was merely that virtual currency was being used. Officials told reporters they were looking into 1,000 transactions by 400 customers. Shortly thereafter, another trading platform, INBRTC, closed its doors, citing a fear that it would run afoul of India's vague currency laws as well. Since then, startups have been cautious to move ahead on anything related to alternative electronic money, because of what's perceived as a crackdown. It's worth noting that while researching India's take on virtual currencies, I kept running into the same pop-up ad below. It only strengthened the case that the country needs a faster payment system.

Most other countries have been quietly watching virtual currencies. Australia's tax office has asked citizens to keep detailed records, but it's otherwise hands-off. Hong Kong, Indonesia, New Zealand, South Korea, and Taiwan haven't made any significant announcements or rulings. In Malaysia, Bitcoin ATMs are being passed off as voucher-spitting vending machines, so the government doesn't mind. And while the Bank of Thailand initially ruled Bitcoin illegal in the summer of 2013, it later became apparent it only did so because the concept didn't fit neatly within its existing laws. Exchanges remained open anyway.

CHAPTER 11

Do Androids Dream of Electric Money?

WE'VE SPENT this entire book taking a look at what Bitcoin is like today. But what about the future? What's in store for credit cards and paper cash? The concept of a truly digital currency with a complex, cryptographic ledger is so revolutionary and has so many implications for finance, art, and everyday life that it's worth exploring what might happen in the days ahead. I've molded together all of the perspectives I received interviewing Bitcoin enthusiasts, cryptographers, hackers, economists, and bankers into one possible vision of the future. Don't think of it as my own fantasy or expectations. Rather, consider this a journey down a single road, one of an infinite number of possibilities. It's an imaginative exercise that forces us to ask: Do we want this to happen, and if not, how can we avert it? Prepare to get jolted a bit. The path that lies ahead is always a rocky one.

The year is—never mind. I'd rather not say. Sometime in the not-too-distant future. It's been 10 years since we last heard of Bitcoin. It had a good run. There was a brief period when everyone thought it was the hottest investment around, and an estimated 50 million people owned at least a portion of a bitcoin, mostly through 401k retirement funds and investment trusts. But then the worst happened. A militaristic group of highly sophisticated hackers developed a nasty piece of malware and wormed their way into the computers of Bitcoin's core developers. It wasn't their fault. These talented coders were the helpless victims of a cyber assault. They had been doing this volunteer work of maintaining the Bitcoin system for years, but like most open-source projects, the whole enterprise was severely underfunded. And so it came that still-unidentified hackers stole the administrator credentials of several Bitcoin developers, secretly logged into their computers, sabotaged Bitcoin's code and sent out the update to every computer on the network. The block chain was corrupted, and therefore, rendered useless. Some people claimed they still had the "real" block chain on their computers, but too many different version of the block chain existed, so no one could be sure which version was the right one. The world mourned the passing of a financial phenomenon, and millions of people lost money. Retirees were furious at their financial consultants, and anyone who mentioned the word "Bitcoin" was generally considered a jerk. It wasn't particularly devastating for any one nation, but it hurt.

In its wake, however, Bitcoin transformed the way we pay one another. The days when restaurants and shops had only a handful of payment networks to choose from—Visa, MasterCard—are long gone. Now there are a half dozen other networks that do the same thing, and all of them work on vast, interconnected peer-to-peer systems. Each one has its own version of a block chain, logging transactions and checking to make sure they add up. In the back room of every shop or restaurant, there's the loud hum of a computer fan. The desktop computer runs full-time, hooked up to a network and verifying the transactions going on all over that network. It costs each business about $200 a month in electricity, but that's nothing compared to the savings it's getting.

The increased competition and low cost of processing transactions has put pressure on payment networks to lower their fees, so now major credit card companies only charge business owners 1 percent on every purchase. A business that makes $1 million in revenue was previously paying those processers $30,000 a year in merchant fees, but now that's down to $10,000. Restaurants have passed those savings along to patrons, and now that it's slightly cheaper to eat out, people do it more often. Waiters and waitresses get the feeling they've been making more money lately, but they're not quite sure. They haven't seen cash—or touched a paper note—in ages. All their tips and their daily paycheck go straight to their digital wallets.

Daily paychecks? That's right. Because transaction fees everywhere have fallen, restaurants don't mind paying their employees on a daily basis. At first it didn't seem like it would matter to get paid $150 a day instead of $1,500 every two weeks. But as it turns out, this makes everyday living a lot easier. Grandparents tell horror stories about how, back in their day, they would pray that a major bill wouldn't be due on a Thursday because they got paid their lump sum on a Friday.

As for spending your money, it's a breeze. Everyone has a digital wallet, and it keeps all money in U.S. dollars or whatever your national currency is. Moving yourself to a different electronic currency just turns out to be a complicated extra step no average person cares to do. Leave that to business owners and their payment networks. But there's added security, because the whole system still uses private keys to access money and public keys to receive it. By now, though, private keys get activated by using a thumbprint or iris scan, so there's no worry about losing access to your money.

That's the most fundamental way that our concept of money has changed. There's no longer this crude notion of carrying around heavy metal coins or stacks of paper. In fact, that seems ridiculous now, when you think about it. Money is not what you have in your possession. It's all about the record of transactions that lives on a community's network. So when a family's house burns down and they lose everything they own—including the mobile devices that "stored" their electronic U.S. dollars—they don't have to worry. They didn't lose their money after all. Somewhere on the shared payment network, there's a record that shows they still have their savings. All they have to do is access another device and use their thumbprint to reactivate their private keys and get back their money, because it never truly lived on their devices. It was always on the backbone of the system. It's just like those days on the island of Yap. It didn't matter that a family lost its stone. Everyone respected the fact that they had a certain amount of wealth. We've transcended our obsession with physicality.

It has also become the age of micropayments. Everyone seems to be paying everyone else a little bit of money all the time. The expenses never seem outrageous, so not very many people complain about it. For instance, most news online doesn't come free any more. Sure, you can read anything you want free of charge from your local tabloid blog, but then you have to deal with all those annoying pop-up commercials that play for 90 seconds straight before you can read a single story. On the other hand, you can't read a single article on a major news site like the *New York Times, Wall Street Journal,* or *Washington Post* without paying first. But you don't mind, because your Web browser does it automatically for you. At the end of the day, you see the $1.20 bill, and you shrug it off as the cost of a single newspaper subscription.

Musicians, graphic artists, and fiction writers don't take the same approach with strict website paywalls. They all let you enjoy their work for free, but they always ask for microtip donations. You happen to be a kind person, so you've set your browser to donate 10¢ for every song you listen to. This kind of overwhelming community support has forever altered what it means to be an artist. Independent musicians feel less pressure to write entire albums with songs that all sound the same. Every song can stand on its own and draw its own financial support, so every piece of music is its own exploration into a thought or a feeling. The lines between genres like rock, jazz, and hip-hop are blurred. Your favorite musical artist is a relatively unknown classical violinist in Toronto who occasionally lends her talents to a metal band in Seattle. They split the microtips on their latest song. It's not a lot, but it's better than having your song copied repeatedly and pirated by everyone.

The situation is the same for self-funded illustrators. A small team of part-time artists in New Mexico has sketched out an emotionally complex, beautifully drawn comic book and distributed it for free. But enough donations came in from fans during the first few weeks that they all quit their day jobs and have started doing this full-time. It's all thanks to people like you. Each time you see a funny online comic strip or entertaining video, you click on the MicroPay button and it automatically deducts another 10¢ from your account. You'd think this sort of constant tipping is expensive. To a certain extent, it is. But you've already decided to cut your television cable bill, and now you only pay for the shows and movies you want to watch. And besides, you've got a small stream of income coming in from Big Data companies.

Does that sound strange? Well, ever since the U.S. Congress approved the Direct Attribution and True Atonement Act, companies that collect your personal information and use it to extract value have to be transparent about how they used that data—and they have to compensate you for some of that. For example, if you're a hospital nurse and your professional activities were carefully analyzed to create a robotic hospital assistant, the DATA Act requires that the robotics company pay you for contributing to that expertise. After all, there's always the chance those new robots might replace you as a worker, so the return seems fair.

But enough with micropayments. The Bitcoin legacy lives on in other ways—some good, some creepy. Governments are now closer than ever to an Orwellian surveillance state, in that they keep track of everyone's movements. The federal government will claim that it does not physically track any innocent Americans without a warrant. It does, however, keep an ongoing database—a block chain, if you will—that tracks every person's entry and exit from a jurisdiction. Whenever someone enters or leaves a city, state, or nation, the movement gets logged in a digital file that gets encoded. The next wave of collected movement data gets built on top of the last one. That means if the government ever wants to look back in time, it can access a permanent record of everyone's whereabouts. The act of stacking the data in a chain of blocks makes it impossible to fake a past data entry without ruining all the data that came in later. The downside is obvious: The government is in a perpetual state of spying on everyone. But there's an upside too: If you ever get wrongfully accused of a crime, you now have a perfect alibi. Plus, no one can steal your identity and use it as a passport or driver's license. You can't be in two places at once, so the impostor should get caught immediately.

The taxpayers also benefit, because they now have 100 percent certainty that all foreign aid is being used exactly the way it was intended. The money is programmable, and rules are written into its code so that it is only spent on a specific good. No matter how much that right-wing South American president hates the socialist movement that's gaining steam in the rural villages, he can't take the $50 million U.S. aid package he just received for flood victims and use it instead to arm paramilitary goons. The money just won't work that way. Frustrated, he spends the electronic aid money on medicine and doctors, which pleases the leftist villagers who then reward him with political support. It's a peaceful outcome, and the U.S. government avoids financially supporting another bloodbath.

Back in the United States, taxpayers also celebrate that fact that, with digital money, they can now track every politician's campaign donations and spending on a public ledger that's viewable online. If your congressman just received a $100,000 donation from an oil drilling company, everyone knows about it. And if he just received 100 donations each worth $1,000, it's easy to find out if they all came from executives at the oil drilling company. The information is publicly available, and it doesn't take a lot of legal wrangling to get those records. If the congressman is ever stupid enough to spend $200 of that money on hookers, everyone knows about it the next day.

To revel in this new era, finance and economics nerds celebrate two holidays on Halloween. It's also Satoshi Day, and fans around the world wear masks that depict the face of that poor old man who was once fingered as the true Satoshi Nakamoto. It's now a tradition to point at anyone who wears the mask and shout, "You're Satoshi!" Fun times.

CHAPTER 12

Final Thoughts

THE WORLD has rarely reacted kindly to revolutionary ideas and technology—especially when it deals with money. In Ancient Greece, Sparta was a militaristic state that had no use for money and the individual empowerment it signified. When the Spartans conquered Mantinea during the Peloponnesian War, they rid the city of its coins and abolished all forms of currency. More than a millennium later, medieval merchants found practicing fractional-reserve banking (having less cash on hand than the total of deposits) were threatened with beheadings. When the French scholar Nicolas Oresme suggested to the king in 1360 that money is not his royal property but that of the people who use it, he was ignored.

Bitcoin faces an uphill battle. Its very design threatens to wrestle away control from governments and banks, two of our most entrenched institutions. It has to overcome our resistance to a concept of money that isn't physical. And like any new contraption, it's unproven and therefore doesn't yet deserve our trust. It's too early to say if Bitcoin is the currency of the future.

But that doesn't mean we should just shrug this off as some trite hobby for tech-savvy Libertarians. Bitcoin takes a stab at solving problems most of us ignore: lack of access to money, high transaction costs, and forced reliance on trusted middle-men. These aren't societal glitches we can afford to disregard. They're holding us back from progressing together. The gap between the rich and poor continues to widen. Leaving behind the unbanked and saddling them with fees for moving their own money has the dangerous potential to destabilize our social framework. Left unattended, these will be a stain on human history.

Then there's the matter that our handling of money has not caught up with the digital age. We interact with money in a digital format—checking bank accounts online, shopping via websites, and paying in person with our smartphones. But behind that digital format is still an archaic system that's dreadfully slow and wasteful of resources. The most marketed banking innovation of the last few years is that we can now snap photos to deposit checks on the go. Shouldn't we stop to ask why we're still using paper checks? The waste is everywhere. The United States government spent 9.6¢ to produce each dollar bill in 2011.[1] That doesn't sound like much until you consider the social cost. In a single year, the government spent $614 million just to print money—funds that could have gone to schools, inner-city programs, and scientific research. And it redirected tons of raw cotton away from more useful products like clothing, increasing the demand and raising the price for the rest of us.

And for what? Our obsession for a physical bill we can point to and call money? For nearly 2,500 years, every king and president has dealt with the problems of coinage, assessing the cost of forging little metal tokens and increasing or decreasing their purity to satisfy a desire based on an arbitrary measure of value. That innocuous craving launched crusades with the Arab world and brutal colonial pillaging throughout Asia,

Africa, and the Americas. Yet it was all based on a ruse. Our fixation with paper and gold and silver is a vast game of misdirection. Money is not about the tokens we have in our possession. It's the system of debt and credit, the IOUs that make up for our lack of trust in one another to trade with a legitimate object of value. Bartering doesn't cut it, so we decide to trust tokens instead. And we don't even do this consciously. It's not malevolent. We're simply filling a gap with an object. But we're better than that.

The Pacific islanders of Yap had it right all along. There's no way to tell if they designed their own system of currency in such a ridiculous way—with those massive, sometimes immovable stones—to prove a point. But even if it was unintentional, the wisdom was there. The moment of truth came when the powerful family lost its stone but still had its wealth recognized by the other villagers. Wealth is what the community says it is, because money is whatever the community says it is. It's a matter of faith.

However, the concept of government-mandated fiat money shows that it's also a matter of assertion. If a powerful enough force says it's money, then it's money. And in a democratic society, if enough people agree that it's money, then it's money. It can be a self-fulfilling prophecy. Bitcoin's toughest challenge is overcoming our doubts and gaining a large enough user base to sustain it. For that, Bitcoin must prove itself worthy of our confidence.

Bitcoin's dual personality disorder doesn't help. Speculative investors who treat it as a commodity make it too volatile to be a stable unit of value, and therefore a good currency. You can't have it both ways. Also, the software that supports the entire protocol can be easily replicated. The system has no inherent competitive advantage over any other digital currency. That means any day now, Wells Fargo can launch its own FargoCoin. Bank of America can create BOApay. Nothing stops JPMorgan Chase from marketing MorganMoney. The typical defense from Bitcoin enthusiasts is that Bitcoiners aren't just going to ditch their beloved currency for big bank inventions. But in reality, the Bitcoin community is tiny. If any one of these banks draws 5 percent of the United States, it will immediately over-shadow the entire Bitcoin community.

I brought this point up to Barry Silbert, the entrepreneur who launched the Bitcoin Investment Trust, and he noted that it's not a fair comparison. This scenario doesn't just require people who own bitcoins migrating away from the digital cur-rency. Silbert argued that there are already hundreds of mil-lions of dollars invested on top of the Bitcoin network—apps, machinery, services—and banks will have a tough time recre-ating that. Maybe that's true.

Then there's what I keep hearing from Silicon Valley folks who think themselves soothsayers. They compare Bitcoin's incredible technology to innovative breakthroughs like email, smartphones, and the automobile. But no one owns this tech-nology. Email was great. Where's the first ever popular email cli-ent now? What about instant messaging service? Smartphone maker? Let's look further back. First car? I wouldn't advise anyone to invest their savings in Bitcoin for the same reason I oppose inflationary policies by central banks run amuck. Hard-earned money deserves to retain its value.

However, Bitcoin the currency deserves a chance. Satoshi Nakamoto, whoever that is, created something that is sheer genius. And in turn, those who continue to build on that idea are doing a great service to society. Whether or not this expedi-tion fails, it's worth a shot. That's why I'll suggest this: If you're brave, go buy a bitcoin—or a fraction of one. Experiment. See how it works. Get a taste for the cutting edge. An invention of this sort has been long overdue in the digital age. We've been talking about this sort of thing for more than a decade.

On July 25, 1995, a few members of Congress walked into Room 2128 at the Rayburn House Office Building in Washington, DC, to discuss the future of money. They listened to testimony from Visa, MasterCard International, Intuit, and two virtual money companies that later flopped. They discussed the lack of banking access for the poor, the high cost of sending money, the trouble of maintaining physical money, and the potential for electronic payments to better regulate welfare payments. Visa expressed apprehension about electronic money that's "nothing more than zeros and ones." Little has changed since.

It's worth noting that one witness, DigiCash CEO David Chaum, said something that might resonate in the post-Bitcoin world: "What would be a real mistake would be to move to an electronic payment system that is fully traceable, where you would be stepping backwards. You would be moving away from the kinds of privacy that people have an expectation of today into a totally transparent world...it would create really the kind of world which many of us have fought to prevent."

If something like Bitcoin succeeds, the question for us then will be whether the benefit of a digital currency outweighs the risk.

Bitcoin: A Peer-to-Peer Electronic Cash System

Satoshi Nakamoto
satoshin@gmx.com
www.bitcoin.org

Abstract. A purely peer-to-peer version of electronic cash would allow online payments to be sent directly from one party to another without going through a financial institution. Digital signatures provide part of the solution, but the main benefits are lost if a trusted third party is still required to prevent double-spending. We propose a solution to the double-spending problem using a peer-to-peer network. The network timestamps transactions by hashing them into an ongoing chain of hash-based proof-of-work, forming a record that cannot be changed without redoing the proof-of-work. The longest chain not only serves as proof of the sequence of events witnessed, but proof that it came from the largest pool of CPU power. As long as a majority of CPU power is controlled by nodes that are not cooperating to attack the network, they'll generate the longest chain and outpace attackers. The network itself requires minimal structure. Messages are broadcast on a best effort basis, and nodes can leave and rejoin the network at will, accepting the longest proof-of-work chain as proof of what happened while they were gone.

1. Introduction

Commerce on the Internet has come to rely almost exclusively on financial institutions serving as trusted third parties to process electronic payments. While the system works well enough for most transactions, it still suffers from the inherent weaknesses of the trust based model. Completely non-reversible transactions are not really possible, since financial institutions cannot avoid mediating disputes. The cost of mediation increases transaction costs, limiting the minimum practical transaction size and cutting off the possibility for small casual transactions, and there is a broader cost in the loss of ability to make non-reversible payments for nonreversible services. With the possibility of reversal, the need for trust spreads. Merchants must be wary of their customers, hassling them for more information than they would otherwise need. A certain percentage of fraud is accepted as unavoidable. These costs and payment uncertainties can be avoided in person by using physical currency, but no mechanism exists to make payments over a communications channel without a trusted party.

What is needed is an electronic payment system based on cryptographic proof instead of trust, allowing any two willing parties to transact directly with each other without the need for a trusted third party. Transactions that are computationally impractical to reverse would protect sellers from fraud, and routine escrow mechanisms could easily be implemented to protect buyers. In this paper, we propose a solution to the double-spending problem using a peer-to-peer distributed timestamp server to generate computational proof of the chronological order of transactions. The system is secure as long as honest nodes collectively control more CPU power than any cooperating group of attacker nodes.

2. Transactions

We define an electronic coin as a chain of digital signatures. Each owner transfers the coin to the next by digitally signing a hash of the previous transaction and the public key of the next owner and adding these to the end of the coin. A payee can verify the signatures to verify the chain of ownership.

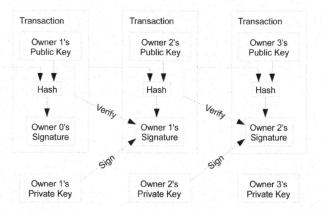

The problem of course is the payee can't verify that one of the owners did not double-spend the coin. A common solution is to introduce a trusted central authority, or mint, that checks every transaction for double spending. After each transaction, the coin must be returned to the mint to issue a new coin, and only coins issued directly from the mint are trusted not to be double-spent. The problem with this solution is that the fate of the entire money system depends on the company running the mint, with every transaction having to go through them, just like a bank.

We need a way for the payee to know that the previous owners did not sign any earlier transactions. For our purposes, the earliest transaction is the one that counts, so we don't care about later attempts to double-spend. The only way to confirm the absence of a transaction is to be aware of all transactions. In the mint based model, the mint was aware of all transactions and decided which arrived first. To accomplish this without a trusted party, transactions must be publicly announced [1], and we need a system for participants to agree on a single history of the order in which they were received. The payee needs proof that at the time of each transaction, the majority of nodes agreed it was the first received.

3. Timestamp Server

The solution we propose begins with a timestamp server. A timestamp server works by taking a hash of a block of items to be timestamped and widely publishing the hash, such as in a newspaper or Usenet post [2-5]. The timestamp proves that the data must have existed at the time, obviously, in order to get into the hash. Each timestamp includes the previous timestamp in its hash, forming a chain, with each additional timestamp reinforcing the ones before it.

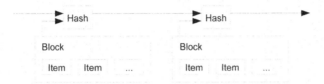

4. Proof-of-Work

To implement a distributed timestamp server on a peer-to-peer basis, we will need to use a proof-of-work system similar to Adam Back's Hashcash [6], rather than newspaper or Usenet posts. The proof-of-work involves scanning for a value that when hashed, such as with SHA-256, the hash begins with a number of zero bits. The average work required is exponential in the number of zero bits required and can be verified by executing a single hash.

For our timestamp network, we implement the proof-of-work by incrementing a nonce in the block until a value is found that gives the block's hash the required zero bits. Once the CPU effort has been expended to make it satisfy the proof-of-work, the block cannot be changed without redoing the work. As later blocks are chained after it, the work to change the block would include redoing all the blocks after it.

The proof-of-work also solves the problem of determining representation in majority decision making. If the majority were based on one-IP-address-one-vote, it could be subverted by anyone able to allocate many IPs. Proof-of-work is essentially one-CPU-one-vote. The majority decision is represented by the longest chain, which has the greatest proof-of-work effort invested in it. If a majority of CPU power is controlled by honest nodes, the honest chain will grow the fastest and outpace any competing chains. To modify a past block, an attacker would have to redo the proof-of-work of the block and all blocks after it and then catch up with and surpass the work of the honest nodes. We will show later that the probability of a slower attacker catching up diminishes exponentially as subsequent blocks are added.

To compensate for increasing hardware speed and varying interest in running nodes over time, the proof-of-work difficulty is determined by a moving average targeting an average number of blocks per hour. If they're generated too fast, the difficulty increases.

5. Network

The steps to run the network are as follows:

1) New transactions are broadcast to all nodes.
2) Each node collects new transactions into a block.
3) Each node works on finding a difficult proof-of-work for its block.
4) When a node finds a proof-of-work, it broadcasts the block to all nodes.
5) Nodes accept the block only if all transactions in it are valid and not already spent.
6) Nodes express their acceptance of the block by working on creating the next block in the chain, using the hash of the accepted block as the previous hash.

Nodes always consider the longest chain to be the correct one and will keep working on extending it. If two nodes broadcast different versions of the next block simultaneously, some nodes may receive one or the other first. In that case, they work on the first one they received, but save the other branch in case it becomes longer. The tie will be broken when the next proof-of-work is found and one branch becomes longer; the nodes that were working on the other branch will then switch to the longer one.

New transaction broadcasts do not necessarily need to reach all nodes. As long as they reach many nodes, they will get into a block before long. Block broadcasts are also tolerant of dropped messages. If a node does not receive a block, it will request it when it receives the next block and realizes it missed one.

6. Incentive

By convention, the first transaction in a block is a special transaction that starts a new coin owned by the creator of the block. This adds an incentive for nodes to support the network, and provides a way to initially distribute coins into circulation, since there is no central authority to issue them. The steady addition of a constant of amount of new coins is analogous to gold miners expending resources to add gold to circulation. In our case, it is CPU time and electricity that is expended.

The incentive can also be funded with transaction fees. If the output value of a transaction is less than its input value, the difference is a transaction fee that is added to the incentive value of the block containing the transaction. Once a predetermined number of coins have entered circulation, the incentive can transition entirely to transaction fees and be completely inflation free.

The incentive may help encourage nodes to stay honest. If a greedy attacker is able to assemble more CPU power than all the honest nodes, he would have to choose between using it to defraud people by stealing back his payments, or using it to generate new coins. He ought to find it more profitable to play by the rules, such rules that favour him with more new coins than everyone else combined, than to undermine the system and the validity of his own wealth.

7. Reclaiming Disk Space

Once the latest transaction in a coin is buried under enough blocks, the spent transactions before it can be discarded to save disk space. To facilitate this without breaking the block's hash, transactions are hashed in a Merkle Tree [7][2][5], with only the root included in the block's hash. Old blocks can then be compacted by stubbing off branches of the tree. The interior hashes do not need to be stored.

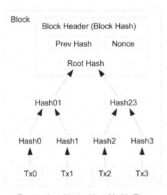

Transactions Hashed in a Merkle Tree

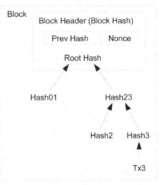

After Pruning Tx0-2 from the Block

A block header with no transactions would be about 80 bytes. If we suppose blocks are generated every 10 minutes, 80 bytes * 6 * 24 * 365 = 4.2MB per year. With computer systems typically selling with 2GB of RAM as of 2008, and Moore's Law predicting current growth of 1.2GB per year, storage should not be a problem even if the block headers must be kept in memory.

8. Simplified Payment Verification

It is possible to verify payments without running a full network node. A user only needs to keep a copy of the block headers of the longest proof-of-work chain, which he can get by querying network nodes until he's convinced he has the longest chain, and obtain the Merkle branch linking the transaction to the block it's timestamped in. He can't check the transaction for himself, but by linking it to a place in the chain, he can see that a network node has accepted it, and blocks added after it further confirm the network has accepted it.

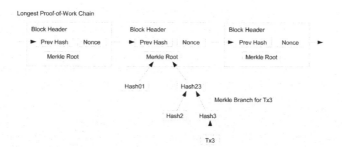

Longest Proof-of-Work Chain

As such, the verification is reliable as long as honest nodes control the network, but is more vulnerable if the network is overpowered by an attacker. While network nodes can verify transactions for themselves, the simplified method can be fooled by an attacker's fabricated transactions for as long as the attacker can continue to overpower the network. One strategy to protect against this would be to accept alerts from network nodes when they detect an invalid block, prompting the user's software to download the full block and alerted transactions to confirm the inconsistency. Businesses that receive frequent payments will probably still want to run their own nodes for more independent security and quicker verification.

9. Combining and Splitting Value

Although it would be possible to handle coins individually, it would be unwieldy to make a separate transaction for every cent in a transfer. To allow value to be split and combined, transactions contain multiple inputs and outputs. Normally there will be either a single input from a larger previous transaction or multiple inputs combining smaller amounts, and at most two outputs: one for the payment, and one returning the change, if any, back to the sender.

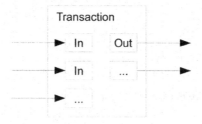

It should be noted that fan-out, where a transaction depends on several transactions, and those transactions depend on many more, is not a problem here. There is never the need to extract a complete standalone copy of a transaction's history.

10. Privacy

The traditional banking model achieves a level of privacy by limiting access to information to the parties involved and the trusted third party. The necessity to announce all transactions publicly precludes this method, but privacy can still be maintained by breaking the flow of information in another place: by keeping public keys anonymous. The public can see that someone is sending an amount to someone else, but without information linking the transaction to anyone. This is similar to the level of information released by stock exchanges, where the time and size of individual trades, the "tape", is made public, but without telling who the parties were.

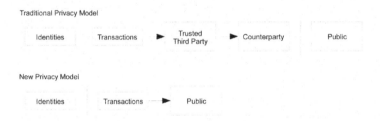

As an additional firewall, a new key pair should be used for each transaction to keep them from being linked to a common owner. Some linking is still unavoidable with multi-input transactions, which necessarily reveal that their inputs were owned by the same owner. The risk is that if the owner of a key is revealed, linking could reveal other transactions that belonged to the same owner.

11. Calculations

We consider the scenario of an attacker trying to generate an alternate chain faster than the honest chain. Even if this is accomplished, it does not throw the system open to arbitrary changes, such as creating value out of thin air or taking money that never belonged to the attacker. Nodes are not going to accept an invalid transaction as payment, and honest nodes will never accept a block containing them. An attacker can only try to change one of his own transactions to take back money he recently spent.

The race between the honest chain and an attacker chain can be characterized as a Binomial Random Walk. The success event is the honest chain being extended by one block, increasing its lead by +1, and the failure event is the attacker's chain being extended by one block, reducing the gap by -1.

The probability of an attacker catching up from a given deficit is analogous to a Gambler's Ruin problem. Suppose a gambler with unlimited credit starts at a deficit and plays potentially an infinite number of trials to try to reach breakeven. We can calculate the probability he ever reaches breakeven, or that an attacker ever catches up with the honest chain, as follows [8]:

p = probability an honest node finds the next block

q = probability the attacker finds the next block

q_z = probability the attacker will ever catch up from z blocks behind

$$q_z = \begin{cases} 1 & \text{if } p \leq q \\ (q/p)^z & \text{if } p > q \end{cases}$$

Given our assumption that $p > q$, the probability drops exponentially as the number of blocks the attacker has to catch up with increases. With the odds against him, if he doesn't make a lucky lunge forward early on, his chances become vanishingly small as he falls further behind.

We now consider how long the recipient of a new transaction needs to wait before being sufficiently certain the sender can't change the transaction. We assume the sender is an attacker who wants to make the recipient believe he paid him for a while, then switch it to pay back to himself after some time has passed. The receiver will be alerted when that happens, but the sender hopes it will be too late.

The receiver generates a new key pair and gives the public key to the sender shortly before signing. This prevents the sender from preparing a chain of blocks ahead of time by working on it continuously until he is lucky enough to get far enough ahead, then executing the transaction at that moment. Once the transaction is sent, the dishonest sender starts working in secret on a parallel chain containing an alternate version of his transaction.

The recipient waits until the transaction has been added to a block and z blocks have been linked after it. He doesn't know the exact amount of progress the attacker has made, but assuming the honest blocks took the average expected time per block, the attacker's potential progress will be a Poisson distribution with expected value:

$$\lambda = z \frac{q}{p}$$

To get the probability the attacker could still catch up now, we multiply the Poisson density for each amount of progress he could have made by the probability he could catch up from that point:

$$\sum_{k=0}^{\infty} \frac{\lambda^k e^{-\lambda}}{k!} \cdot \begin{cases} (q/p)^{(z-k)} & \text{if } k \leq z \\ 1 & \text{if } k > z \end{cases}$$

Rearranging to avoid summing the infinite tail of the distribution...

$$1 - \sum_{k=0}^{z} \frac{\lambda^k e^{-\lambda}}{k!} \left(1 - (q/p)^{(z-k)} \right)$$

Converting to C code...

```
#include <math.h>
double AttackerSuccessProbability(double q, int z)
{
    double p = 1.0 - q;
    double lambda = z * (q / p);
    double sum = 1.0;
    int i, k;
    for (k = 0; k <= z; k++)
    {
        double poisson = exp(-lambda);
        for (i = 1; i <= k; i++)
            poisson *= lambda / i;
        sum -= poisson * (1 - pow(q / p, z - k));
    }
    return sum;
}
```

Running some results, we can see the probability drop off exponentially with z.

q=0.1
z=0 P=1.0000000
z=1 P=0.2045873
z=2 P=0.0509779
z=3 P=0.0131722
z=4 P=0.0034552
z=5 P=0.0009137
z=6 P=0.0002428
z=7 P=0.0000647
z=8 P=0.0000173
z=9 P=0.0000046
z=10 P=0.0000012

q=0.3
z=0 P=1.0000000
z=5 P=0.1773523
z=10 P=0.0416605
z=15 P=0.0101008
z=20 P=0.0024804
z=25 P=0.0006132
z=30 P=0.0001522
z=35 P=0.0000379
z=40 P=0.0000095
z=45 P=0.0000024
z=50 P=0.0000006

Solving for P less than 0.1%...

P < 0.001
q=0.10 z=5
q=0.15 z=8
q=0.20 z=11
q=0.25 z=15
q=0.30 z=24
q=0.35 z=41
q=0.40 z=89
q=0.45 z=340

12. Conclusion

We have proposed a system for electronic transactions without relying on trust. We started with the usual framework of coins made from digital signatures, which provides strong control of ownership, but is incomplete without a way to prevent double-spending. To solve this, we proposed a peer-to-peer network using proof-of-work to record a public history of transactions that quickly becomes computationally impractical for an attacker to change if honest nodes control a majority of CPU power. The network is robust in its unstructured simplicity. Nodes work all at once with little coordination. They do not need to be identified, since messages are not routed to any particular place and only need to be delivered on a best effort basis. Nodes can leave and rejoin the network at will, accepting the proof-of-work chain as proof of what happened while they were gone. They vote with their CPU power, expressing their acceptance of valid blocks by working on extending them and rejecting invalid blocks by refusing to work on them. Any needed rules and incentives can be enforced with this consensus mechanism.

References

[1] W. Dai, "b-money," http://www.weidai.com/bmoney.txt, 1998.

[2] H. Massias, X.S. Avila, and J.-J. Quisquater, "Design of a secure timestamping service with minimal trust requirements," In *20th Symposium on Information Theory in the Benelux*, May 1999.

[3] S. Haber, W.S. Stornetta, "How to time-stamp a digital document," In *Journal of Cryptology*, vol 3, no 2, pages 99-111, 1991.

[4] D. Bayer, S. Haber, W.S. Stornetta, "Improving the efficiency and reliability of digital time-stamping," In *Sequences II: Methods in Communication, Security and Computer Science*, pages 329-334, 1993.

[5] S. Haber, W.S. Stornetta, "Secure names for bit-strings," In *Proceedings of the 4th ACM Conference on Computer and Communications Security*, pages 28-35, April 1997.

[6] A. Back, "Hashcash—a denial of service counter-measure," http://www.hashcash.org/papers/hashcash.pdf, 2002.

[7] R.C. Merkle, "Protocols for public key cryptosystems," In *Proc. 1980 Symposium on Security and Privacy*, IEEE Computer Society, pages 122-133, April 1980.

[8] W. Feller, "An introduction to probability theory and its applications," 1957.

Notes

Chapter 1: Baby Steps

1   D. Graeber, "NakedCapitalism.com," 13 September 2011. [Online]. Available: http://www.nakedcapitalism.com/2011/09/david-graeber-on-the-invention-of-money-%E2%80%93-notes-on-sex-adventure-monomaniacal-sociopathy-and-the-true-function-of-economics.html.

2   C. Menger, *On the Origins of Money*, 1892.

3   C. University, "The Song Dynasty in China," 2008. [Online]. Available: http://afe.easia.columbia.edu/song/econ/money.htm.

Chapter 2: The Birth of Bitcoin

1   S.L.F.R. Bank, "The Financial Crisis—A Timeline of Event and Policy Actions," [Online]. Available: http://timeline.stlouisfed.org/index.cfm?p=timeline.

2   "Bailout Recipients," 11 March 2014. [Online]. Available: http://projects.propublica.org/bailout/list.

3   Y. Kuznetsov, "Fiat Money as an Administrative Good," *Mises Daily,* 28 April 2010.

4   Michael McLeay, Amar Radia, and Ryland Thomas. "Money Creation in the Modern Economy," *Bank of England Quarterly Bulletin* 2014 Q1 (14 March). Available: http://ssrn.com/abstract=2416234.

5   D. Murdock, "Milton and Rose Friedman Offer Radical Ideas for the 21st Century," *Cato Institute,* 8 December 1999.

6   "SourceForge," [Online]. Available: http://sourceforge.net/p/bitcoin/news/2009/01/bitcoin-v01-released---p2p-e-cash/.

7   A. Peterson, "Hal Finney received the first Bitcoin transaction. Here's how he describes it.," *Washington Post,* 3 January 2014.

8   M.J. Casey, "Bitcoin Foundation's Andresen on Working with Satoshi Nakamoto," *Wall Street Journal,* 6 March 2014.

9   National Institute of Standards and Technology, "CVE-2010-5139," National Vulnerability Database, 2012.

10 M. Sawyer, "Monetarism," 26 February 2013. [Online]. Available: http://www.monetarism.co.uk/the-beginners-guide-to-bitcoin-everything-you-need-to-know/.

11 J. Davis, "The Crypto-Currency," *New Yorker,* 10 October 2011.

12 "History of Bitcoin," [Online]. Available: http://historyofbitcoin.org/.

13 FATF, "Money Laundering Using New Payment Methods," October 2010. [Online]. Available: http://www.fatf-gafi.org/media/fatf/documents/reports/ML%20using%20New%20Payment%20Methods.pdf.

14 J. Brito, "Online Cash Bitcoin Could Challenge Governments, Banks," *Time,* 16 April 2011.

15 A. Jeffries, "My Bitcoin Spokesman Finally Comes Forward," 8 August 2011. [Online]. Available: http://betabeat.com/2011/08/mybitcoin-spokesman-finally-comes-forward-what-did-you-think-we-did-after-the-hack-we-got-shitfaced/.

16 J. Davis, "The Crypto-Currency."

17 A. Penenberg, "The Bitcoin Crypto-currency mystery reopened," 11 October 2013. [Online]. Available: http://www.fastcompany.com/1785445/bitcoin-crypto-currency-mystery-reopened. [Accessed 2011].

18 Christopher Mims and Leo Mirani, "Bitcoin's creator is Japanese mathematician Shinichi Mochizuki, says hypertext inventor," 19 May 2013. [Online]. Available: http://qz.com/86255/the-mysterious-creator-of-bitcoin-could-be-japanese-mathematician-shinichi-mochizuki-says-the-inventor-of-hypertext/.

19 A. Liu, "Who Is Satoshi Nakamoto, the Creator of Bitcoin?," 22 May 2013. [Online]. Available: http://motherboard.vice.com/blog/who-is-satoshi-nakamoto-the-creator-of-bitcoin.

20 L. M. Goodman, "The Face Behind Bitcoin," 6 March 2014. [Online]. Available: http://mag.newsweek.com/2014/03/14/bitcoin-satoshi-nakamoto.html.

Chapter 3: Bitcoin Explained

1 S. Nakamoto, "Bitcoin: A peer-to-peer electronic cash system," 2008.

2 Goldman Sachs Global Investment Research, "All about Bitcoin," Goldman Sachs, New York, 2014.

3 S. Nakamoto, "Bitcoin: A peer-to-peer electronic cash system."

4 Ibid.

5 CoinDesk, "How Bitcoin Mining Works," 6 March 2014. [Online]. Available: http://www.coindesk.com/information/how-bitcoin-mining-works/.

6 Unknown, "Protocol rules," [Online]. Available: https://en.bitcoin.it/wiki/Protocol_rules#cite_ref-5. [Accessed 2 May 2014].

7 S. Nakamoto, "Bitcoin: A peer-to-peer electronic cash system."

8   Bitcoin Foundation, "Block 0," [Online]. Available: http://block
    explorer.com/block/000000000019d6689c085ae165831e934ff763ae46
    a2a6c172b3f1b60a8ce26f. [Accessed 3 May 2014].
9   A.Y.C. Heng, "Global Bitcoin Nodes Distribution," [Online]. Available:
    https://getaddr.bitnodes.io/. [Accessed 3 May 2014].

Chapter 4: Using It in Real Life

1   S. Gibbs, "Man buys $27 of bicoin, forgets about them, finds they're now
    worth $886k," 29 October 2013. [Online]. Available: http://www.the
    guardian.com/technology/2013/oct/29/bitcoin-forgotten-currency-
    norway-oslo-home.
2   R. Orange, "Student buys Osla flat with $27 bitcoin stash," 29
    October 2013. [Online]. Available: http://www.thelocal.no/20131029/
    student-buys-oslo-apartment-with-27-bitcoin-stash.
3   E. Morphy, "Here Is What Bitcoin Users Are Buying On Overstock.
    com," 22 January 2014. [Online]. Available: http://www.forbes.com/
    sites/erikamorphy/2014/01/22/here-is-what-bitcoin-users-are-buying-
    on-overstock-com/.
4   R. Sidel, "Overstock CEO Sees Bitcoin Sales Rising More Than
    Expected," 4 March 2014. [Online]. Available: http://online.wsj.com/
    news/articles/SB10001424052702304815004579418962232488216.
5   M. Andreessen, "Why Bitcoin Matters," 21 January 2014. [Online].
    Available: http://dealbook.nytimes.com/2014/01/21/why-bitcoin-matters/.
6   Winklevoss Bitcoin Trust, Securities and Exchange Commission, 2014.

Chapter 5: But Is It Money?

1   G. Mankiw, *Macroeconomics*, New York: Worth Publishers, 2007.
2   R.A. Ferdman, "Venezuela's black market rate for US dollars just
    jumped by almost 40%," 26 March 2014. [Online]. Available: http://
    qz.com/192395/venezuelas-black-market-rate-for-us-dollars-just-
    jumped-by-almost-40/.
3   William Henry Furnace III, *The Island of Stone Money: Uap of the Caro-
    lines*, J.B. Lippincott Company, 1910.
4   F. Martin, *Money: The Unauthorized Biography*, New York: Alfred A.
    Knopf, 2014.
5   N. Ferguson, *The Ascent of Money*, New York: Penguin Books, 2008.
6   F. Martin, *Money: The Unauthorized Biography*.
7   P.L.P. Simpson, *The Politics of Aristotle*, University of North Carolina
    Press, 1997.

8   F. Martin, *Money: The Unauthorized Biography.*

9   P.L.P. Simpson, *The Politics of Aristotle.*

10 "Matthew 22:15-22," in the Holy Bible.

11 J. Peden, "Inflation and the Fall of the Roman Empire," 7 September 2009. [Online]. Available: https://mises.org/daily/3663.

12 N. Ferguson, *The Ascent of Money.*

13 Ibid.

14 F. Martin, *Money: The Unauthorized Biography.*

15 Ibid.

16 A.G. Kenwood and A.L. Lougheed, *The Growth of the International Economy 1820–2000*, New York: Routledge, 1999.

17 Ibid.

18 Jim O'Donoghue, Louise Goulding, and Grahame Allen, "Consumer Price Inflation Since 1750," Office for National Statistics. Economic Trends, 2004.

19 Federal Reserve Bank of Minneapolis, "Consumer Price Index, 1913–," [Online]. Available: https://www.minneapolisfed.org/community_education/teacher/calc/hist1913.cfm. [Accessed 27 April 2014].

20 N. Ferguson, *The Ascent of Money.*

21 A.G. Kenwood and A.L. Lougheed, *The Growth of the International Economy 1820–2000.*

22 L.E. Lehrman, *The True Gold Standard*, Lehrman Institute, 2012.

23 G. Mankiw, *Macroeconomics*, New York: Worth Publishers, 2007.

24 U.S. Federal Reserve, "Is U.S. currency still backed by gold?," [Online]. Available: http://www.federalreserve.gov/faqs/currency_12770.htm. [Accessed 26 April 2014].

25 S. Dinan, "U.S. debt jumps a record $328 billion—tops $17 trillion for first time," 18 October 2013. [Online]. Available: http://www.washingtontimes.com/news/2013/oct/18/us-debt-jumps-400-billion-tops-17-trillion-first-t/.

26 Central Bank of Malta, "Coinage of the Knights of Malta," [Online]. Available: http://www.centralbankmalta.org/site/currency1b.html. [Accessed 27 April 2014].

Chapter 6: The Case for Bitcoin

1   U.S. Census Bureau, "2008-2012 American Community Survey 5-Year Estimates," 2012.

2   DCF, "Temporary Assistance for Needy Families—An Overview of Program Requirements," 2006.

3   C. Megerian, "Banks profit from fees paid by California welfare recipients," March 25 2014. [Online]. Available: http://articles.latimes. com/2014/mar/25/local/la-me-welfare-fees-20140326.

4   FDIC, "National Survey of Unbanked and Underbanked Households," 2011.

5   L. Mandel, "The Financial Literacy of Young American Adults," Jump$tart, Washington, DC, 2006.

6   C. Bell, "Check cashing still not a good deal," 18 November 2011. [Online]. Available: http://www.bankrate.com/financing/banking/ check-cashing-still-not-a-good-deal/.

7   S. Hargreaves, "15% of Americans living in poverty," 17 September 2013. [Online]. Available: http://money.cnn.com/2013/09/17/news/economy/ poverty-income/.

8   J. Ross, "Banks Extract Fees On Unemployment Benefits," 1 November 2011. [Online]. Available: http://www.huffingtonpost.com/2011/11/01/ bank-fees-unemployment-benefits_n_1033700.html.

9   Jessica Silver-Greenberg and Stephanie Clifford, "Paid via Card, Workers Feel Sting of Fees," 30 June 2013. [Online]. Available: http://www. nytimes.com/2013/07/01/business/as-pay-cards-replace-paychecks-bank-fees-hurt-workers.html.

10 Pew Research Internet Project, "Mobile Technology Fact Sheet," January 2014. [Online]. Available: http://www.pewinternet.org/fact-sheets/ mobile-technology-fact-sheet/.

11 M. Duggan, "Pew Internet Resource Project," 19 September 2013. [Online]. Available: http://www.pewinternet.org/2013/09/19/cell-phone-activities-2013/.

12 D. Henry, "JPMorgan Chase plans to exit prepaid card business," 9 January 2014. [Online]. Available: http://www.reuters.com/article/ 2014/01/09/us-jpmorgan-cards-prepaid-idUSBREA080XM20140109.

13 Leora Klapper and Krita Hoff, "Half of Adults Worldwide Report Having a Formal Bank Account," Gallup, 2012.

14 Al Jazeera, "UN: 460,000 displaced in Darfur this year," 14 November 2013. [Online]. Available: http://www.aljazeera.com/news/africa/ 2013/11/un-displaced-violence-darfur-2013111413261056629.html.

15 K. DeYoung, "U.S. sends Osprey aircraft, more Special Operations forces to hunt Ugandan warlord," 23 March 2014. [Online]. Available: http://www.washingtonpost.com/world/national-security/2014/03/23/ aa468ca6-b2d0-11e3-8020-b2d790b3c9e1_story.html.

16 Jenny Aker and Isaac Mbiti, "Mobile Phones and Economic Development in Africa," *Journal of Economic Perspectives*, 2010.

17 K. Yeoman, "M-PESA helps world's poorest go to the bank using mobile phones," 6 January 2014. [Online]. Available: http://www.csmonitor. com/World/Making-a-difference/Change-Agent/2014/0106/M-PESA-helps-world-s-poorest-go-to-the-bank-using-mobile-phones.

18 GSMA, "Safaricom—Kenya—Feasibility Study," 2012.

19 William Jack and Tavneet Suri, "The Economics of M-PESA," Working paper, http://www.mit.edu/~tavneet/M-PESA-Final.pdf. August 2010.

20 I. Mas and O. Morawczynski, "Designing Mobile Money Services—Lessons from M-PESA," *MIT Press Journals*, 2009.

21 Megan G. Plyler, Sherri Haas, and Geetha Nagarajan, "Community-Level Economic Effects of M-PESA in Kenya: Initial Findings," Iris Center, University of Maryland, 2010.

22 GSMA, "Mobile Economy Latin America," 2013.

23 Leora Klapper and Krita Hoff, "Half of Adults Worldwide Report Having a Formal Bank Account," Gallup, 2012.

24 B. Williams, "Using mobile to reach the Latin American unbanked," 1 August 2012. [Online]. Available: http://bankinganalyticsblog.fico.com/2012/08/using-mobile-to-reach-the-latin-american-unbanked-.html.

25 IDB, "Remittances in Latin America by the Numbers," 2011. [Online]. Available: http://www.iadb.org/en/topics/remittances/by-the-numbers, 2584.html.

26 JPMorgan Chase Bank, "United States Patent Application 20130317984," 5 August 2013. [Online]. Available: http://appft.uspto. gov/netacgi/nph-Parser?Sect1=PTO2&Sect2=HITOFF&p=1&u= %2Fnetahtml%2FPTO%2Fsearch-bool.html&r=1&f=G&l=50&co1 =AND&d=PG01&s1=20130317984&OS=20130317984&RS=20130317984.

27 R. Edmonds, "ASNE census finds 2,600 newsroom jobs were lost in 2012," 25 June 2013. [Online]. Available: http://www.poynter.org/latest-news/business-news/the-biz-blog/216617/asne-census-finds-2600-newsroom-jobs-were-lost-in-2012/.

28 "PayPal Merchant Fees," [Online]. Available: https://www.paypal.com/webapps/mpp/merchant-fees#id1_header. [Accessed 18 April 2014].

29 R. Edmonds, "ASNE census finds 2,600 newsroom jobs were lost in 2012."

30 Chicago Sun-Times, "Chicago Sun-Times Now Accepting Bitcoin Payments," 3 April 2014. [Online]. Available: http://www.prweb.com/releases/2014/04/prweb11733314.htm.

31 B. Cunningham, "Bitcoin Talk forum," 15 May 2012. [Online]. Available: https://bitcointalk.org/index.php?topic=81858.0.

32 "BTC Tip," [Online]. Available: https://secure.btctip.com:9000/. [Accessed 19 April 2014].

33 E. Garland, "The 'In Rainbows' Experiment: Did It Work?," 16 November 2009. [Online]. Available: http://www.npr.org/blogs/monitormix/2009/11/the_in_rainbows_experiment_did.html.

34 S. Michaels, "In Rainbows outsells last two Radiohead albums," 16 October 2008. [Online]. Available: http://www.theguardian.com/music/2008/oct/16/radiohead-album-sales.

35 Amanda Palmer, *The Art of Asking*. TED talk, February 2013. [Performance]. Available: http://www.ted.com/talks/amanda_palmer_the_art_of_asking/transcript.

36 K.A. Davidson, "Jamaican Bobsledders Ride Dogecoin Into Olympics," 4 February 2014. [Online]. Available: http://www.bloombergview.com/articles/2014-02-04/jamaican-bobsledders-ride-dogecoin-into-olympics.

37 N. Kwan, "OfficeMax Sends Letter to "Daughter Killed in Car Crash"," 19 January 2014. [Online]. Available: http://www.nbcchicago.com/news/local/OfficeMax-Sends-Letter-to-Daughter-Killed-in-Car-Crash-240941291.html.

38 B. Krebs, "U.S. States Investigating Breach at Experian," 3 April 2014. [Online]. Available: http://krebsonsecurity.com/2014/04/u-s-states-investigating-breach-at-experian/.

39 M. Martin, "Experian and Court Ventures data breach," 7 April 2014. [Online]. Available: http://www.usinfosearch.com/Experian-Court-Ventures-Data-Breach.html.

40 A. Greenberg, "Follow the Bitcoins: How We Got Busted Buying Drugs on Silk Road's Black Market," 5 September 2013. [Online]. Available: http://www.forbes.com/sites/andygreenberg/2013/09/05/follow-the-bitcoins-how-we-got-busted-buying-drugs-on-silk-roads-black-market/. [Accessed 2013].

41 S. Meiklejohn, "A Fistful of Bitcoins: Characterizing Payments Among," Association for Computing Machinery, 2013.

42 Matthew Rosenberg and Azam Ahmed, "U.S. Aid to Afghans Flows on Despite Warnings of Misuse," 30 January 2014. [Online]. Available: http://www.nytimes.com/2014/01/30/world/asia/report-says-afghanistan-cant-be-trusted-to-prevent-misuse-of-us-aid.html.

43 A. Ibrahim, "U.S. Aid to Pakistan—U.S. Taxpayers Have Funded Pakistani Corruption," Belfer Center for Science and International Affairs, Harvard Kennedy School of Government, 2009.

44 Huffington Post UK, "British Aid Money To Sierra Leone Investigated After Claims Of Misuse," 15 April 2013. [Online]. Available: http://www.huffingtonpost.co.uk/2013/04/15/sierra-leone-aid-money_n_3083057.html.

45 G. Selgin, "Milton Friedman and the Case against Currency Monopoly," *Cato Journal*, 2008.

46 Federal Reserve Bank of Dallas, "Hyperinflation in Zimbabwe," 2011.

47 Economic Times, "Zimbabwe inflation now over 1 million percent," 13 June 2008. [Online]. Available: http://articles.economictimes.indiatimes.com/2008-06-13/news/27696937_1_zimbabwe-inflation-zimbabwe-dollars-harare.

48 Economist, "A century of decline," 15 February 2014. [Online].Available: http://www.economist.com/news/briefing/21596582-one-hundred-years-ago-argentina-was-future-what-went-wrong-century-decline.

49 J. Parker, "Case of the Day: Money and Inflation in Argentina," [Online]. Available: http://academic.reed.edu/economics/parker/f10/201/cases/argentina.html. [Accessed 21 April 2014].

Chapter 7: The Case against Bitcoin

1   D. Gage, "The Venture Capital Secret: 3 Out of 4 Start-Ups Fail," 20 September 2012. [Online]. Available: http://online.wsj.com/news/articles/SB10000872396390443720204578004980476429190.

2   U.S. Census Bureau, "American Time Use Survey," 2012.

3   Harris Interactive, "Most Americans Still Don't Trust Bitcoin Despite Widespread Awareness, New Survey Shows," 25 March 2014. [Online]. Available: http://www.webwire.com/ViewPressRel.asp?aId=186455#.U1aoL_ldWuk.

4   Caltech, "Independent discovery by George Zweig," [Online]. Available: http://hep.caltech.edu/gm/gm.php?p=zweig.php. [Accessed 22 April 2014].

5   G. Richmond, "Special 301: FOSS users. Now we're all Communists and Criminals," 5 March 2010. [Online]. Available: http://www.freesoftwaremagazine.com/articles/special_301_foss_users_now_were_all_communists_and_criminals.

6   F.R. Velde, "Bitcoin: A primer," The Federal Reserve Bank of Chicago, Chicago, 2013.

7   L. Orsini, "What Happens to Lost Bitcoins?," 13 January 2014. [Online]. Available: http://readwrite.com/2014/01/13/what-happens-to-lost-bitcoins#awesm=~oCeplYWFrRAv06.

8   "Buffett blasts bitcoin as 'mirage': 'Stay away!'," 14 March 2014. [Online]. Available: http://www.cnbc.com/id/101494937.

Chapter 8: The Rise and Fall of Mt.Gox

1   Ripple, "Interview with Jed McCaleb, inventor of the Ripple protocol and co-founder of OpenCoin," 17 April 2013. [Online]. Available: https://ripple.com/blog/interview-with-jed-mccaleb-inventor-of-the-ripple-protocol-and-co-founder-of-opencoin/.

2   R. McMillan, "Bitcoin Maverick Returns for New Crack at Digital Currency," 30 September 2013. [Online]. Available: http://www.wired.com/2013/09/jed_mccaleb/.

3   "Internet Archive," [Online]. Available: https://web.archive.org/web/20070525044536/http://mtgox.com/gwt/mtgox.php. [Accessed 25 May 2007].

4   "Internet Archive," [Online]. Available: https://web.archive.org/web/20090812073342/http://www.mtgox.com/. [Accessed 12 August 2009].

5   J. McCaleb, "Bitcoin Talk," 18 July 2010. [Online]. Available: https://bitcointalk.org/index.php?topic=444.0;all.

6   M. Karpelès, "blog.magicaltux.net," 9 June 2009. [Online]. Available: https://web.archive.org/web/20090609223038/http://blog.magicaltux.net/.

7   M. Karpelès, "Bitcoin Talk," 8 November 2010. [Online]. Available: https://bitcointalk.org/index.php?action=profile;u=2134;sa=show Posts;start=0.

8   "Bitcoin Charts," [Online]. Available: http://bitcoincharts.com/charts/mtgoxUSD#tgSzm1gi0zm2g25zvzcv. [Accessed 9 April 2014].

9   "Banque de France," 8 June 2013. [Online]. Available: http://vosdroits.service-public.fr/particuliers/F2417.xhtml#N10131.

10 "Mt.Gox AMA," 12 April 2013. [Online]. Available: http://www.reddit.com/r/Bitcoin/comments/1c7ahh/we_are_mt_gox_ama.

11 13-1085SAG. U.S. District Court of Maryland, 19 June 2013.

12 13-1162SKG. U.S. District Court of Maryland, 14 August 2013.

13 *Coinlab v. Mt.Gox, Tibanne,* 2013.

14 R. Dillet, "Feds Seize Another $2.1 Million From Mt. Gox, Adding Up To $5 Million," 23 August 2013. [Online]. Available: http://

techcrunch.com/2013/08/23/feds-seize-another-2-1-million-from-mt-gox-adding-up-to-5-million/.

15　R. McMillan, "The Inside Story of Mt. Gox, Bitcoin's $460 Million Disaster," 3 March 2014. [Online]. Available: http://www.wired.com/2014/03/bitcoin-exchange/.

16　Coinbase, "Joint Statement Regarding Mt.Gox," 24 February 2014. [Online]. Available: http://blog.coinbase.com/post/77766809700/joint-statement-regarding-mtgox.

17　Unknown, "Crisis Strategy Draft," 2014.

18　"Domain Report—GoX.com," Domain Tools, 2014.

Chapter 9: The Dark Side of Bitcoin

1　J. Finkle, "Marketplace of vice, 'Silk Road' meets its end," 2 October 2013. [Online]. Available: http://www.reuters.com/article/2013/10/02/us-crime-silkroad-marketplace-idUSBRE99I1CP20131002.

2　A. Hern, "FBI struggles to seize 600,000 Bitcoins from alleged Silk Road founder," 7 October 2013. [Online]. Available: http://www.theguardian.com/technology/2013/oct/07/fbi-bitcoin-silk-road-ross-ulbricht.

3　*United States of America v. Ross William Ulbricht,* 2013.

4　B. Krebs, "U.S.: Online payment network abetted fraud, child pornography," 1 May 2007. [Online]. Available: http://www.washingtonpost.com/wp-dyn/content/article/2007/05/01/AR2007050101291.html.

5　J. Langlois, "Liberty Reserve digital money service shut down, founder arrested," 27 May 2013. [Online]. Available: http://www.globalpost.com/dispatch/news/business/technology/130527/liberty-reserve-digital-money-service-shut-down-founder-arrested.

6　F. Berkman, "Alleged Silk Road drug 'kingpin' is actually just a 'digital landlord,' says lawyer," 1 April 2014. [Online]. Available: http://www.dailydot.com/news/silk-road-ross-ulbricht-digital-landlord-bitcoin/.

7　Digital Citizens Alliance, "Busted, but not broken—The state of Silk Road and the Darknet marketplaces," Digital Citizens Alliance, 2014.

Chapter 10: How Governments Are Responding

1　Internal Revenue Service, "Notice 2014-21," 2014.

2　A. Levitin, "Bitcoin Tax Ruling," 26 March 2014. [Online]. Available: http://www.creditslips.org/creditslips/2014/03/bitcoin-tax-ruling.html.

3　Johannes Schmidt, Alexander Derrick, and Joseph Henchman, "IRS Says Bitcoin to Be Taxed as Gains; New Rule Is Retroactive," [Online].

Available: http://taxfoundation.org/blog/irs-says-bitcoin-be-taxed-gains-new-rule-retroactive.

4   New York Labor Department, "Number of Nonfarm Jobs by Place of Work," 2014.

5   Goldman Sachs, 2014.

6   B. Rooney, "U.S. Treasury continues to probe Standard Chartered," 8 August 2012. [Online]. Available: http://buzz.money.cnn.com/2012/08/08/treasury-probe-standard-chartered/.

7   K. Mahbubani, "A Lawsky unto himself, or why New York erred on StanChart," 12 August 2012. [Online]. Available: http://webcache.googleusercontent.com/search?q=cache:u6MaLjOEGBsJ:www.ft.com/cms/s/0/f4c6b142-e2d5-11e1-bf02-00144feab49a.html+&cd=1&hl=en&ct=clnk&gl=us#axzz2xz0q0Ry2.

8   European Commission, "Life Online," 2012.

9   Morgunblaðið, "Höftin stöðva viðskipti með Bitcoin," 19 December 2013. [Online]. Available: http://www.mbl.is/vidskipti/frettir/2013/12/19/hoftin_stodva_vidskipti_med_bitcoin/.

10   L. Tung, "Auroracoin begins cryptocurrency 'airdrop' to whole of Iceland," 25 March 2014. [Online]. Available: http://www.zdnet.com/auroracoin-begins-cryptocurrency-airdrop-to-whole-of-iceland-7000027676/.

11   General Prosecutor of the Russian Federation, "General Prosecutor's Office of the Russian Federation held a meeting on the legitimacy of the use of anonymous payment systems and kriptovalyut," 6 February 2014. [Online]. Available: http://genproc.gov.ru/smi/news/genproc/news-86432/.

12   A. Ostroukh, "Russia Ready to Float Ruble Next Year Regardless of Rate," *The Wall Street Journal,* 17 January 2014.

13   A. Hannestad, "Bitcoin-gevinster kan stikkes direkte i lommen," 25 March 2014. [Online]. Available: http://politiken.dk/oekonomi/dkoekonomi/ECE2244816/bitcoin-gevinster-kan-stikkes-direkte-i-lommen/.

14   J. Wild, "Alderney looks to cash in on virtual Bitcoins with Royal Mint reality," *The Financial Times,* 29 November 2013.

15   CBC, "Bitcoins aren't tax exempt, Revenue Canada says," 26 March 2014. [Online]. Available: https://ca.finance.yahoo.com/news/bitcoins-arent-tax-exempt-revenue-canada-says-134047396--finance.html.

16   Julie Gordon and Leah Schnurr, "Canadian police investigating after bitcoin bank Flexcoin folds," 5 March 2014. [Online]. Available:

http://www.reuters.com/article/2014/03/06/us-bitcoin-flexcoin-idUSBREA2503F20140306.

17 Forbes, "Banxico advierte sobre el uso del Bitcoin," 10 March 2014. [Online]. Available: http://www.forbes.com.mx/sites/banxico-advierte-sobre-el-uso-del-bitcoin/.

18 El Espectador, "Alerta por Bitcoin en Colombia," 25 March 2014. [Online]. Available: http://www.elespectador.com/noticias/economia/alerta-bitcoin-colombia-articulo-483080.

19 Banco Central do Brasil, "PRESS RELEASE NO. 25,306," 19 February 2014. [Online]. Available: https://www3.bcb.gov.br/normativo/detalharNormativo.do?method=detalharNormativo&N=114009277.

20 Economist, "Bitcoin paradise," 25 December 2013. [Online]. Available: http://www.economist.com/blogs/schumpeter/2013/12/libertarian-enclaves.

21 AP, "Vietnam says Bitcoin transactions are illegal," 28 February 2014. [Online]. Available: http://bigstory.ap.org/article/vietnam-says-bitcoin-transactions-are-illegal.

22 C. Fuller, "Singapore Taxes Bitcoin: How New Taxation May Be Exactly What Bitcoin Needs," 13 January 2014. [Online]. Available: http://www.ibtimes.com/singapore-taxes-bitcoin-how-new-taxation-may-be-exactly-what-bitcoin-needs-1538142.

23 Monami Yui and Takahiko Hyuga, "Japan Says Bitcoin Not Currency Amid Calls for Regulation," 7 March 2014. [Online]. Available: http://www.bloomberg.com/news/2014-03-07/japan-says-bitcoin-is-not-a-currency-amid-calls-for-regulation.html.

24 Goldman Sachs Global Investment Research, "All about Bitcoin," Goldman Sachs, New York, 2014.

25 P. Mishra, "First time in India bitcoin traders raided in Ahmedabad," 27 December 2013. [Online]. Available: http://timesofindia.indiatimes.com/business/india-business/First-time-in-India-bitcoin-traders-raided-in-Ahmedabad/articleshow/28008526.cms.

Chapter 12: Final Thoughts

1 Parija Kavilanz, "Guess What? Dollar Bills Are Made of Cotton." 8 March 2011. [Online]. Available: http://money.cnn.com/2011/03/08/news/economy/dollar_cotton_prices.